The Ethical Practice of Psychology in Organizations

The Ethical Practice of Psychology in Organizations

Edited by Rodney L. Lowman

Section Editors

Scott L. Martin
Larry Fogli

Casebook Contributing Editors

David W. Bracken
Steven H. Brown
Gary B. Brumback
Nita R. French
Sharon Green
Geula G. Lowenberg
John R. Murray
Lance W. Seberhagen
Nancy T. Tippins
John R. Turner
Kristina Whitney
R. Stephen Wunder

Distinguished Case Review Panel

Douglas W. Bray
Kenneth E. Clark
Leaetta M. Hough

Chairpersons, Professional Practice Committee
Society for Industrial and Organizational Psychology

Walter W. Tornow
A. Catherine Higgs

AMERICAN PSYCHOLOGICAL ASSOCIATION · WASHINGTON, DC
SOCIETY FOR INDUSTRIAL AND ORGANIZATIONAL PSYCHOLOGY · BOWLING GREEN, OH

Copyright © 1998 by the American Psychological Association and the Society for Industrial and Organizational Psychology, Inc. All rights reserved. Except as permitted under the United States Copyright Act of 1976, no part of this publication may be reproduced or distributed in any form or by any means, or stored in a database or retrieval system, without the prior written permission of the publisher.

Published by
American Psychological Association
750 First Street, NE
Washington, DC 20002

Society for Industrial and Organizational Psychology, Inc.
745 Haskins Road, Suite D
P.O. Box 87
Bowling Green, OH 43402

Typeset in Century by EPS Group Inc., Easton, MD

Printer: Data Reproductions Corporation, Auburn Hills, MI
Cover designer: Berg Design, Albany, NY
Technical/production editor: Valerie Montenegro

Library of Congress Cataloging-in-Publication Data
The ethical practice of psychology in organizations / edited by Rodney L.
Lowman . . . [et al.].
    p.   cm.
Includes bibliographical references and index.
ISBN 1-55798-486-7 (acid-free paper)
1. Psychology, Industrial.   2. Organizational sociology.   I. Lowman,
Rodney L.
HF5548.8.E79   1998
158.7—dc21
                                                                97-47450
                                                                     CIP

British Library Cataloguing-in-Publication Data
A CIP record is available from the British Library.

Printed in the United States of America
First edition

Contents

Foreword

Ethical issues in the workplace are very complex in an era of global work settings, with multiple legal and social structures and with workers from many cultural backgrounds and varied personal beliefs. We hope that this book will challenge readers to reflect on the ethical implications of their own actions and engage in dialogue with fellow professionals about ethical issues. As the professional organization for psychologists in the world of work, the Society for Industrial and Organizational Psychology, Inc. (SIOP; Division 14 of the American Psychological Association [APA]) has as a primary focus the education of its members—and all human resource professionals—about the ethical dilemmas we all face at work. In that spirit, we are proud to have sponsored this publication and express our deepest thanks to the editor, Dr. Rodney L. Lowman, and his many colleagues for their dedicated work on this book.

On April 13, 1997, the Executive Committee of SIOP voted to endorse the publication of *The Ethical Practice of Psychology in Organizations*. In voting this endorsement, it was not SIOP's intent to present this work as an official policy manual for either SIOP or APA (which it is not, nor do SIOP or APA represent it as such), but rather to recommend the book's use as an excellent set of materials for professional development of psychologists and other human resource professionals.

We hope that each reader finds the book thought-provoking.

KEVIN R. MURPHY
President, 1997–1998
Society for Industrial and
   Organizational Psychology, Inc.

Preface

Call it a character defect if you like, but as a matter of personal preference, temperament, and character structure, I usually enjoy plowing new ground more than reworking a well-tilled plot. After unsuccessfully resisting the "call" for as long as I could, I therefore approached with considerable ambivalence a job I had known for some time needed to be done—one that I had indeed advocated and that I sincerely had hoped would be assumed by someone else this time around. Serving as editor-in-chief for the second edition of the SIOP ethics casebook has in fact turned out to be a much more challenging, formidable, and downright educational task than I imagined. Here's why.

Twelve years ago—has it really been that?—we faced considerable challenge in creating a first ethics casebook (Lowman, 1985) for industrial/organizational (I/O) psychology. The pioneering group that assembled that diverse and still intriguing set of cases courageously surmounted considerable odds—the absence of precedent, of consensus, and of agreement on need—to make that first casebook a reality. SIOP's Executive Committee exercised considerable prescience in sponsoring that project and in distributing the casebook as a benefit of membership to everyone in what was then called APA's Division of I/O Psychology.

Since 1985, when the first casebook was published, I/O psychology has become a far more complex profession than the first casebook reflected. Not only have the guiding ethical parameters undergone a major overhaul, but I/O psychology is a much more advanced field than it was a decade ago. For one thing, there is considerably more technical knowledge, and for another, there are many more practitioners using I/O psychology in an increasingly wondrous diversity of settings and applications. By any standard, I/O psychology is a flourishing and expanding enterprise.

This revised casebook includes a significant update of many of the original cases (several hardly recognizable from their original form) and what I think you will agree is an exciting assortment of new cases reflecting contemporary issues in the practice of I/O psychology. As before, our goal was not to provide an ethics "cookbook" in which the answer to every ethical dilemma could instantly be obtained, but to offer one resource for stimulating the process of thinking ethically about I/O psychology in all its contemporary diversity. Then and now, we intentionally avoided didactic instruction and detailed ethical or theoretical references, leaving that task for ethical theorists and for other books and articles.

The casebook rather provides true-to-life examples from the "firing line" (a bad metaphor perhaps for those denizens of a downsized corporate America) of types of circumstances that practitioners and researchers alike can and do encounter. Some of these cases are fictional or composites, but many are masked renderings of real-life examples generously provided to us by the SIOP membership. In the casebook review process, it was at times amusing for me to hear someone comment that a particular case was simply not realistic or likely to happen in real life when I knew that the case had actually been based on a similar real-life episode. As a veteran of service on the APA Ethics Committee, I urge caution in pronouncing any—and I do mean *any*—professional behavior as being beyond the realm of realistic possibility.

The practice of I/O psychology today, perhaps inevitably, occurs in an ever-increasingly complex and at times litigious environment. It is therefore important to state clearly and for the record that the opinions about and applications of the APA Ethical Principles contained in this book are simply those of the authors and editors and do not constitute official policy of any group, board, or body, including SIOP or APA, the copublishers of this volume. Although these cases are believed to be consistent with APA policy and interpretations and have been carefully reviewed by a variety of experts prior to publication, the applications cited here are meant to stimulate awareness of ethical issues, not to make policy or to define ethical behavior. The case discussions are not statements of APA or its Ethics Committee or of SIOP. On the contrary, the entire casebook is meant to be educational, not a treatise defining obligatory, minimal, or enforceable standards of practice. Any citations of this casebook in the forensic context should always make these caveats known. Psychologists and psychologists-in-training desiring to obtain official opinions of the APA Ethics Committee should consult statements issued by that body.

Ethical applications often create controversy and, if they successfully teach anything, will incite disagreement among equally well-intended professionals. A desired outcome of this casebook is not that each reader agree with every case interpretation—only the most banal set of cases would produce that outcome—but rather that the cases inspire discussion, debate, and more routine, more complex consideration of the ethics of I/O psychology. Ethics, after all, is one of the few defining characteristics of this or any other profession.

Finally, as we now know from personal experience, ethics codes change with time, as do parameters of professional practice. Although this casebook is a good-faith effort to reflect what is known about governing ethical parameters as of this writing, it is unlikely that all cases or applications will continue to be valid over time. Assuring the currency of ethical practice is the responsibility of each professional who aspires to practice ethically.

RODNEY L. LOWMAN

Acknowledgments

Only those who have worked intensively on professional publications that are the product of voluntary associations can fully appreciate the challenges in creating and disseminating such documents. Without the considerable efforts of a wide-ranging group of associates of diverse talents, such undertakings never come to life or else would, as too often happens, die prematurely.

In producing this new edition of the I/O casebook, I am pleased to have had the assistance of many people, both from within SIOP and without. Of particular help were those hard-working section editors and casebook panelists who worked with borrowed time and considerable diligence to make this product a reality. The names of the members of the Committee are shown on the title page of this volume. I would particularly like to single out from among these members the excellent contributions of the distinguished review panel, Douglas Bray (other than me, the only surviving member of the original casebook development effort), Kenneth Clark (who continued to provide review and input despite having had serious personal challenges during the project), and Leaetta Hough (whose support and enthusiasm are gratefully acknowledged).

A number of outside reviewers provided helpful commentary on earlier drafts of this volume. These included Wendy Becker, James Farr, Carl Greenberg, Edward Pavur, Neal Schmitt, Walt Tornow, and the entire SIOP Executive Committee. Lee Hakel helped coordinate many aspects of the project, including coordinating with SIOP's Executive Committee.

I need to single out for special recognition and thanks a number of individuals from SIOP. Walt Tornow was one of the initial instigators of the casebook revision effort. He invited me to resume the editorship, provided considerable help in the initial phases of the project, and was always a hugely supportive force to whom I could turn for guidance and support. Catherine Higgs, who served as Chair of the Professional Affairs Committee throughout the last half of this project, proved to be an exceptionally capable project administrator. Despite her own considerable personal challenges that coincided with this project, Cathy helped successfully negotiate an agreement between SIOP and APA Books, worked closely with SIOP's Executive Committee on a variety of issues affecting the project, and kept me and my committee on target and motivated despite many challenges to the project's completion. Her negotiating and administrative oversight skills proved invaluable.

SIOP's Executive Committee was exceptionally supportive throughout the project. I have worked with a number of professional association governing groups over the years, but few can rival SIOP's in its professionalism and ability to handle complex projects well and with a minimum of inappropriate intrusion. It was the SIOP Executive Committee that agreed—readily—to the suggestion that, as with the first version of the casebook, a copy of the revised casebook be distributed to SIOP members at its expense as a benefit of membership.

Against some resistance, I persisted in advocating that this project be a joint publishing effort of SIOP and APA Books. I felt that APA Books was the best publisher for this document because of its strong list in ethics and because it would help to assure that the volume was distributed to non-I/O psychologists who might be practicing or considering practicing in the field. As one who has been involved in shepherding several documents through the elaborate APA approval process, I well knew that in working with this publisher, there would be both in-house legal and Ethics Office reviews of a very detailed nature. I wish to acknowledge publicly the excellent contributions to the review process of Stanley E. Jones (Director of APA's Office of Ethics) and Nathalie Gilfoyle (APA's Deputy General Counsel). At first I was opposed to the very detailed review that Stan Jones and Nathalie Gilfoyle proposed to provide, but in time I came to see that these reviews have been very beneficial to this volume. Stan Jones in particular helped to assure that we did not make unwarranted assumptions about the applicability of the code in particular cases and that the document reflected how the APA Ethics Code is practically applied. I am very grateful.

I would also like to thank several members of the APA Books staff, including Mary Lynn Skutley, Julia Frank-McNeil, and Peggy Schlegel, for their support and advice. Valerie Montenegro proved to be a skilled production editor.

We received case contributions from many SIOP members and others. We could not use them all, but we appreciated every one of them. Case contributors included Richard Barrett, Wendy Becker, Parschal Baute, Martin Bruce, Michael Campion, Ira Levin, Edward Pavur, Lisa Saari, and Vicki Vandaveer. Additionally, the Casebook Contributing Editors and Section Editors contributed many cases.

Vicki Vandaveer also served as Chair of the Professional Practice Committee during part of the time the casebook was in preparation. I also thank SIOP Presidents Michael Campion, James L. Farr, and Kevin Murphy, and the SIOP Executive Committees, for their support and assistance in making the casebook a reality.

My family (Linda and Marissa) suffered through this project's production with their usual tolerance and good cheer. It is always a pleasure to acknowledge their support.

This casebook was completed over the course of a geographic relocation and survived modern technology crises, including a hard drive crash or two. If I have inadvertently omitted anyone who should have been thanked, I apologize, but please know that your contribution helped make a difference.

RODNEY L. LOWMAN

The Ethical Practice of Psychology in Organizations

Part I

Personnel Selection

Case 1 ⸻⸻⸻⸻⸻⸻⸻⸻⸻⸻

Assessment Techniques

A. Statement of the Problem

A large manufacturer asked an industrial/organizational (I/O) psychologist to develop a selection battery for jobs requiring unskilled employees in one of its plants. The management's goal was to select employees who were average, or below average, in intelligence. The presumption was that this would lead to less turnover, since these employees would have fewer employment options.

A battery consisting of three cognitive tests was recommended by the psychologist and implemented by the firm's personnel department. The battery was administered to applicants with the usual instructions. Applicants were selected whose scores were above a rather low minimal threshold and at or below the average performance on the test. No feedback was provided to the persons assessed on how their test scores were used in the selection process. Unsuccessful high-scoring applicants who inquired about their performance were led to assume that they had not performed well on the screening tests. Requests for specific feedback were turned down.

B. Ethics Code Standards[1]

Ethical Standard 1.07 Describing the Nature and Results of Psychological Services

(a) When psychologists provide assessment, evaluation, treatment, counseling, supervision, teaching, consultation, research, or other psychological services to an individual, a group, or an organization, they provide, using language that

---

[1]These and all subsequent citations from the Ethical Principles of Psychologists and Code of Conduct (American Psychological Association [APA], 1992) are here reproduced with the permission of the publisher, the American Psychological Association. This book does not represent an official interpretation of the APA Ethics Code or an official statement by the Society for Industrial and Organizational Psychology, APA, the APA Ethics Committee, or any APA governance body. Standards are abbreviated with ellipses (...) to emphasize the relevance for the organizational context and the particular case. The full text of the APA Ethics Code is found in the Appendix.

is reasonably understandable to the recipient of those services, appropriate information beforehand about the nature of such services and appropriate information later about results and conclusions.

Ethical Standard 2.03   Test Construction

Psychologists who develop and conduct research with tests and other assessment techniques use scientific procedures and current professional knowledge for test design, standardization, validation, reduction or elimination of bias, and recommendations for use.

Ethical Standard 2.02   Competence and Appropriate Use of Assessments and Interventions

(a) Psychologists who develop, administer, score, interpret, or use psychological assessment techniques, interviews, tests, or instruments do so ... in light of the research on or evidence of the usefulness and proper application of the techniques.

Ethical Standard 6.06   Planning Research

(a) Psychologists design, conduct, and report research in accordance with recognized standards of scientific competence and ethical research.
(b) Psychologists plan their research so as to minimize the possibility that results will be misleading.
(c) In planning research, psychologists consider its ethical acceptability under the Ethics Code. If an ethical issue is unclear, psychologists seek to resolve the issue....
(d) Psychologists take reasonable steps to implement appropriate protections for the rights and welfare of ... participants....

C. Case Interpretation

This case involves the responsibility of the psychologist to maintain competence in the development and use of assessment techniques and the appropriate manner of dealing with job candidates. A major issue raised by the case is the lack of job analysis and validation, with an almost certainly negative reaction of high-scoring applicants were they to learn of the methodology used for selection.

No job analytic validation study was done in this case. Instead, the psychologist recommended a procedure that only appeared, without evidence, to be relevant. To test the company's assertion that average or below average candidates are less likely to quit would have required the empirical demonstration of a negative relationship between the test score and turnover. Since there was no empirical evidence to support this contention, and since the psychologist failed even to go to the literature to consider whether this issue had previously been addressed, the psychologist behaved in an inappropriate manner.

There are also technical problems associated with the psychologist's approach. Applicants and test takers reasonably assume that doing well on a test is the desired direction. It is questionable whether candidates should be misled by not informing them of changes to the usual test-taking assumptions. Yet, were candidates told in advance of the manner in which the test was to be used, there is no evidence of the effects on validity of administering an employment test with these revised instructions.

Furthermore, even if the relationship between job tenure and cognitive test scores had been empirically demonstrated to be negative, the impact of the proposed selection procedure on other aspects of performance needs also to be considered. Other potentially relevant criteria included safety, quality of work, and the ability to learn new tasks quickly.

D. Case Implications

Requests for assistance with selection procedures are often made without the inquiring organization's full understanding of the legal and technical issues involved. Psychologists should be able to communicate to clients the relevant legal and technical aspects of selection in terms the organizational representatives can understand.

Second, the client organization's decision makers need to be made aware of the psychologist's ethical responsibilities in personnel selection. When the demands of the organization create an ethical conflict, the psychologist should clarify for the organization's representatives the ethical position that is considered professionally proper. Finally, psychologists must themselves struggle with ethically ambiguous issues and attempt to resolve conflicts among ethical and technical standards in a way that minimizes harm to all parties.

Case 2 —————————————————

Validation Efforts With Small Sample Sizes

A. Statement of the Problem

A consulting psychologist was approached by a company to develop a new procedure for use in selecting sales personnel. The company wanted the new procedure to replace a nonvalidated, off-the-shelf sales aptitude instrument it was then using. This test had been developed by a human resources executive and was based upon its author's theory of there being a relationship between biorhythms, among other factors it purported to measure, and sales success. There was no empirical research to support this theory, it had not been validated at the employment site, and the author could provide no validation or other research that had been performed on the selection device.

Based on his evaluation of the company's existing selection procedure, the psychologist agreed to develop and validate a new selection procedure. After conducting a job analysis of the sales position, he and his team developed a biographical data inventory. The new inventory key was empirically derived from a concurrent validation study by comparing responses of the 10 best performing sales personnel with those of the 10 poorest performing incumbents. The company employed only 37 salespeople. Moreover, its turnover was very low, resulting in only 1 or 2 new hires per year. Using a rather low criterion of statistical significance ($p < .10$), the consultant developed the scoring key by selecting those items and item alternatives that showed a statistically significant difference between high and low performers. In the project's validation report, the consultant recommended the use of the biographical data inventory in making future selection decisions.

The consultant included in the validation report a caveat that the company should cross-validate the scoring key in the future but did not explain to the company what "cross-validation" was or why it was important. Since the company did not employ an in-house psychologist to make this interpretation, the cross-validation study never occurred.

B. Ethics Code Standards

Ethical Standard 1.07   Describing the Nature and Results of Psychological Services

9

(a) When psychologists provide . . . consultation, research, or other psychological services to . . . an organization, they provide, using language that is reasonably understandable to the recipient of those services, appropriate information beforehand about the nature of such services and appropriate information later about results and conclusions.

Ethical Standard 1.14   Avoiding Harm

Psychologists take reasonable steps to avoid harming their patients or clients, research participants, students, and others with whom they work, and to minimize harm where it is foreseeable and unavoidable.

Ethical Standard 2.02   Competence and Appropriate Use of Assessments and Interventions

(a) Psychologists who develop, administer, score, interpret, or use psychological assessment techniques, interviews, tests, or instruments do so . . . in light of the research on or evidence of the usefulness and proper application of the techniques.

Ethical Standard 2.03   Test Construction

Psychologists who develop and conduct research with tests and other assessment techniques use scientific procedures and current professional knowledge for test design, standardization, validation, reduction or elimination of bias, and recommendations for use.

Additionally, the Society for Industrial and Organizational Psychology's (SIOP) *Principles for the Validation and Use of Personnel Selection Procedures* (1987) specify that "researchers should guard against overestimates of validity resulting from capitalization on chance" (p. 16). These *Principles* further specify that "there should be at least presumptive evidence for the validity of a predictor prior to its operational use" (SIOP, 1987, p. 14).

C. Case Interpretation

The two most important factors in this case involve (1) the effects on the well-being of the client organization and job applicants of developing the new selection procedure versus using other selection methods and (2) the psychologist's use of research methods which are known to overstate the operational validity of the selection procedure.

Concerning the first issue, a basic question concerns whether the psychologist should have accepted the consulting assignment at all, given the severely limited sample sizes available and the proposed empirical validation strategy. Before initiating work on the new inventory, the psychologist appropriately evaluated the selection measures currently in use and properly concluded that the current test was probably invalid for its intended purposes and that a new approach would be needed.

With respect to the second issue, however, use of a contrasting groups method of keying biographical data inventory capitalized heavily upon chance. This problem is especially acute when, as was known at the outset of this project to apply to this case, very small sample sizes are used. The problem was further aggravated by use of a relaxed standard for evaluating statistical significance (i.e., $p < .10$). This approach in all likelihood resulted in an inflated estimate of the validity the client could expect when using the new procedure in making selection decisions.

The results should have been cross-validated using a holdout sample to compensate partially for the use of methodologies that capitalized on chance. Unfortunately, the psychologist's admonition in his report to cross-validate the obtained results before implementing the selection procedure was under the described circumstances unlikely to happen. The client presumably had the expectation of obtaining a usable selection procedure upon the completion of the project. A requirement for more data (which, because of the low rate of hiring, would not have become available in any reasonable period of time) before the selection procedure could be released for use was technically correct but practically unlikely to happen.

The psychologist in this case used a concurrent validation strategy when it was technically not feasible. At the least, the psychologist should have planned and conducted the project in ways that would have minimized overstatement of the operational validity the new procedure would have. He also had the professional obligation to inform the client of limitations or pertinent facts about the study that could affect the operational validity of the new selection procedure. In particular, the psychologist needed to inform the client that the methods used were very likely to overstate the validity (and accuracy) of the selection procedure in operational use and that evaluating its validity on a second sample would be highly important. Then, the client's representatives could make an informed decision about whether to implement the program or not.

The psychologist should have recognized the inherent limitations of the particular methodology he employed and should have planned to use other selection strategies that (1) would not produce an overestimate of validity and/or (2) would provide other kinds of evidence of the procedure's validity. One possibility would have been to declare criterion-related validation technically infeasible due to inadequate sample sizes. Then, validation efforts could have focused on content- or construct-oriented methodologies. These methods eliminate the need for cross-validation because they do not capitalize on chance. The psychologist might also have employed an already-validated measure rather than, in effect, creating a new one.

The psychologist could also have augmented the criterion-related validation with other evidence of validity: The knowledge, skills, and abilities identified in the job analysis could have been systematically "mapped" into the contents of the inventory items to provide some content validation support. Existing, well-researched measures pertinent to the constructs being measured in the new inventory could also have been administered during the validation study, and a convergent and discriminant (construct) validity analysis undertaken. The psychologist might also have evaluated the operational validity of the new procedure, given different hypothetical levels of loss of validity, through cross-validation. If, for example, a "worst-case" scenario still showed that there would be good validity remaining, the confidence in the procedure's operational use would be enhanced, while a scenario that showed the validity to decline to an unacceptably low level would lead to the opposite conclusion.

D. Case Implications

Psychologists practicing I/O psychology often confront situations in which the technically correct or ideal is not possible. In such cases, psychologists must educate their clients and potential clients about the inherent limitations and the alternatives which may work best or be most defensible in specific applications. Generally, however, the client cannot be expected to be knowledgeable about the technical issues involved or the alternatives available. It is the psychologist's ethical obligation to assure that the alternatives and risks of alternative courses of action are clearly presented to the client. When a potential client insists on proceeding with a strategy that the psychologist knows to be problematic or misguided, it may be more appropriate to decline an assignment rather than undertake a course of action known to be seriously flawed.

Case 3 _____

Test Validation Strategies

A. *Statement of the Problem*

An I/O psychologist was hired by a plant manager to develop a selection system for supervisors in the plant of a large corporation. Company officials had made clear in the preliminary meetings that they were interested in funding the study only if it could save the organization considerable money. The consultant was keenly aware of the client's considerable pressure to demonstrate the effectiveness of the selection system.

The company employed a total of 450 supervisors. It hired about 15 new persons with master's degrees in business administration (MBAs) and promoted about 15 in-house employees to become supervisors each year. In constructing the selection battery, the psychologist asked company representatives to identify 15 of the best performing and 15 of the worst performing MBAs from the same age group (25–30 years old) as the typical applicant group.

The psychologist then administered an extensive experimental test battery under standardized conditions to each group. The test battery included cognitive ability tests, a situational judgment inventory, a biographical data form that had been developed by the psychologist at another company for a similar position, several projective tests, and a structured interview. All instruments, including the projective tests, were administered by the psychologist's administrative assistant, a recent college graduate who was studying for his master's degree in counseling. In addition, archival data such as grade point average, rank in class, and Graduate Records Examination (GRE) or Graduate Management Admission Test (GMAT) scores were pulled from each employee's personnel file. The entire test battery yielded 85 separate scores for each assessee.

After inspecting the results, the psychologist picked the eight most discriminating scores and then calculated a multiple correlation coefficient for what was then proposed to be the final selection battery. The resulting value was $R = .8$. In an oral presentation to the company's management, the psychologist showed a plot of points based on this result and displayed an expectancy table which indicated 95% accuracy of prediction. The client was enthusiastic about these results but expressed concern that use of the battery might result in too many "eggheads." The psychologist therefore added an additional question to the interview to measure "organizational fit." The company implemented the new testing program within 2 months of the briefing.

B. Ethics Code Standards

Ethical Standard 1.05   Maintaining Expertise

Psychologists who engage in assessment, . . . organizational consulting, or other professional activities maintain a reasonable level of awareness of current scientific and professional information in their fields of activity, and undertake ongoing efforts to maintain competence in the skills they use.

Ethical Standard 1.07   Describing the Nature and Results of Psychological Services

(a) When psychologists provide assessment . . . they provide, using language that is reasonably understandable to the recipient of those services, appropriate information beforehand about the nature of such services and appropriate information later about results and conclusions.

Ethical Standard 1.15   Misuse of Psychologists' Influence

Because psychologists' scientific and professional judgments and actions may affect the lives of others, they are alert to and guard against personal, financial, social, organizational, or political factors that might lead to misuse of their influence.

Ethical Standard 1.22   Delegation to and Supervision of Subordinates

(a) Psychologists delegate to their employees, supervisees, and research assistants only those responsibilities that such persons can reasonably be expected to perform competently, on the basis of their education, training, or experience, either independently or with the level of supervision being provided.

Ethical Standard 2.03   Test Construction

Psychologists who develop and conduct research with tests and other assessment techniques use scientific procedures and current professional knowledge for test design, standardization, validation, reduction or elimination of bias, and recommendations for use.

Ethical Standard 2.05   Interpreting Assessment Results

When interpreting assessment results, including automated

interpretations, psychologists take into account the various test factors and characteristics of the person being assessed that might affect psychologists' judgments or reduce the accuracy of their interpretations. They indicate any significant reservations they have about the accuracy or limitations of their interpretations.

C. Case Interpretation

This case involves questions of sampling, proper communications with clients, the type of research data appropriate for developing a selection system, strategies for validation, administration of various types of tests, and the interpretation of data. The psychologist's behavior was problematic in several respects.

Above all, the psychologist had responsibility for conducting personnel research in accordance with accepted professional standards and governmental guidelines. If the psychologist had adhered to these standards and guidelines for test validation, the need for a job analysis defining the requirements of the job would have been clear. Similarly, the sampling problem created by using the extremes of only one subset of the population typically selected for the position would have been evident. By selecting the 8 most discriminating scores when there were 85 separate scores and only 30 participants representing the two extremes, the psychologist capitalized upon chance. To have designed a project in this way suggests that the psychologist either did not know the statistical limitations of this approach (itself a concern) or knew them and intentionally ignored the inherent problems to further the goal of his procedures looking good in his client's perception. Either course was problematic. A psychologist familiar with selection testing would also have been concerned about using instruments developed and validated for other than their intended purposes as well as properly administering test instruments. Finally, the knowledgeable psychologist should not have been so quick to change a selection procedure with demonstrated validity to one based on unreliable and unvalidated personal judgment.

D. Case Implications

Psychologists need to be aware of potential conflicts that may often be present in organizational research or practice between acting in accordance with sound scientific principles and handling pressures that may arise from clients to present impressive research results. Psychologists should make it clear to their clients before beginning projects such as validation studies that it is possible that their research findings will not support the prior expectations or hopes for dramatically favorable results. When, despite careful job analyses and selection of relevant predictors, personnel validation studies do not support the predictive efficacy of a test battery, or do so only partially, the psychologist has the professional obligation to inform the client of the actual results. In cases of less than stellar validity coefficients, utility analyses might still be used to demonstrate the procedures' effectiveness compared with alternatives which might be even less efficacious. Finally, psychologists working on industrial selection projects must always be aware of, and employ, scientifically appropriate validation strategies.

Case 4 _____

Avoiding Potential Misuse of
Assessment Procedures

A. Statement of the Problem

Two university-based I/O psychologists were contacted for help with a reorganization problem in a medium-size manufacturing company. The company was undergoing a project intended to streamline its operations and improve efficiency by decreasing the number of levels of management and making positions multitask. The company had originally hired a management consulting firm to help in the reengineering. However, the president of the company was concerned that this firm had been unable to provide solutions for the selection and placement of employees in the reorganized company. Therefore, the company decided to contract with the I/O psychologists to develop a new selection/placement procedure for the future jobs in the new structure. This system was to be used to assess and place both current managers and potential new employees.

During the psychologists' first meeting with the president and key members of the management consulting firm, it became clear that the new structure of the company and the proposed jobs were well defined at a conceptual, but not at an operational, level. As a result, the psychologists were concerned that were they to take on the project, they might not be able to use professionally acceptable methods to develop and validate a revised selection and placement system. During the discussion the president also intimated that a major purpose of the reorganization was to remove some of the less productive people in the firm. She indicated that she needed assurance that the psychologists' efforts would result in a more vital and motivated workforce by the end of the project.

The psychologists left the meeting with the strong impression that they were facing an ambiguous but potentially problematic consulting situation and that the restructuring initiative was possibly an excuse to terminate older employees and to replace them with less experienced ones who were perceived to be more motivated and "vital." Based on this interpretation and the uncertainty of the new structure and jobs, the psychologists advised the company that they would not be available to participate in the project because they were too busy. No other feedback was given, nor were any recommendations made on their concerns.

B. Ethics Code Standards

Ethical Standard 1.16   Misuse of Psychologists' Work

(a) Psychologists do not participate in activities in which it appears likely that their skills or data will be misused by others, unless corrective mechanisms are available.

Ethical Standard 2.02   Competence and Appropriate Use of Assessments and Interventions

(b) Psychologists refrain from misuse of assessment techniques, interventions, results, and interpretations and take reasonable steps to prevent others from misusing the information these techniques provide. . . .

Ethical Standard 8.03   Conflicts Between Ethics and Organizational Demands

If the demands of an organization with which psychologists are affiliated conflict with the Ethics Code, psychologists clarify the nature of the conflict, make known their commitment to the Ethics Code, and to the extent feasible, seek to resolve the conflict in a way that permits the fullest adherence to the Ethics Code.

C. Case Interpretation

Psychologists who are asked to develop psychological assessment procedures need to be concerned that those who will be affected by the results of such procedures will be treated appropriately. When there is reasonable cause to believe that the intent of a proposed procedure is unethical and/ or illegal (e.g., violation of such employment legislation as the Age Discrimination in Employment Act), psychologists have a responsibility to inform clients and potential clients of the concern.

In the present case, the psychologists' unelaborated refusal to consult, indicating only that they were "too busy," did not make clear to the company that eliminating more experienced workers and replacing them with less experienced ones might be challenged as an instance of alleged age discrimination, especially if the decisions were based on invalid selection or placement procedures and particularly as it affected employees already in place on jobs. A more ethically appropriate response in the present case might have been to inform the company officials of the potentially negative consequences of the suggested actions and, if otherwise appropriate, to offer to work with management to avoid these problems. For example, the use of validated procedures could have been used to place employees in future jobs that best matched their skills.

A second ethical issue concerns the confusion regarding the proposed new structure and jobs. Although traditional validation procedures may not have been appropriate in this situation (because the jobs were about to change), alternative tools might be available or might have been developed. Instead of declining the consulting contract, and potentially leaving both the company and its employees in a vulnerable position, the psychologists might have reframed the identified issues to find a way to increase the efficiency of the operation while also protecting the obligations to the employees. Part of an I/O psychologist's role in such situations is to help organizations balance competing interests.

D. Case Implications

When approached by a potential client organization for consultation, I/O psychologists should make clear that assessment procedures will be developed only according to professionally acceptable standards. Consulting I/O psychologists can, as in this case, be placed in a position in which the demands of the client organization are in conflict with relevant ethical standards and/or legal guidelines. In such cases, it is the responsibility of the psychologist to recognize these situations before agreeing to accept a consulting assignment. If the psychologist determines that there is an ethical/legal conflict, the nature of the conflict (or apparent conflict) should be explained clearly to the organization's representatives. Because I/O psychologists can be especially vulnerable to requests by organizational representatives to use psychological assessment procedures for inappropriate purposes, they need to be continuously alert to potential abuses. In such cases, psychologists strive to educate clients and to work to develop an appropriate vision that will also meet stated needs.

I/O psychologists who work as practitioners are constantly faced with situations that are ambiguous, require methods to be adapted to fit client needs, involve potential conflicts of interest, or potentially violate ethical or legal principles. Neither avoidance of nor colluding with possibly illegal actions is an appropriate course of action. Psychologists' roles include educating clients and potential clients to understand the full ramifications of proposed actions and helping them find alternative solutions to potentially illegal or unethical behavior.

Case 5

Mis-Keyed Test Items on Commercially Marketed Tests

A. Statement of the Problem

In the process of reviewing a test developed and sold by a major test publisher, an I/O psychologist discovered that the intended correct answer to a test had been incorrectly keyed. The psychologist consulted several knowledgeable experts, who concurred that the item was mis-keyed. The psychologist then called this error to the attention of a high-ranking psychologist employed by the test-publishing company.

Instead of being interested in improving the test, the official from the test-publishing company verbally abused the test reviewer and subsequently failed to respond to a written request for a change in the scoring key. The publishing company did not make any changes in the test's scoring key and continued to market the test in the usual manner. Because the test was overall the best available one on the market for its purpose, the psychologist continued to use it. To account for the mis-keying, the psychologist changed each response for the mis-keyed item to the "keyed correct" response.

B. Ethics Code Standards

Ethical Standard 2.02   Competence and Appropriate Use of Assessments and Interventions

(a) Psychologists who develop, administer, score, interpret, or use psychological assessment techniques, interviews, tests, or instruments do so in a manner and for purposes that are appropriate in light of the research on or evidence of the usefulness and proper application of the techniques.

Ethical Standard 8.04   Informal Resolution of Ethical Violations

When psychologists believe that there may have been an ethical violation by another psychologist, they attempt to resolve

the issue by bringing it to the attention of that individual if an informal resolution appears appropriate and the intervention does not violate any confidentiality rights that may be involved.

Ethical Standard 8.05   Reporting Ethical Violations

If an apparent ethical violation is not appropriate for informal resolution under Standard 8.04 or is not resolved properly in that fashion, psychologists take further action appropriate to the situation, unless such action conflicts with confidentiality rights in ways that cannot be resolved. Such action might include referral to state or national committees on professional ethics or to state licensing boards.

C. Case Interpretation

The psychologist who developed the test and the responsible or highest ranking psychologist in the test-publishing company bear a professional responsibility for providing test takers and test users with reliable and valid tests. They should provide procedures for questioning the accuracy of the scoring key for individual items.

In this case, the psychologist at the test-publishing company behaved inappropriately by verbally abusing the questioning psychologist while ignoring compelling evidence that a test item was improperly keyed. This was not just a problem of unprofessional behavior, but it also ignored an important responsibility that those who develop and sell tests have to test users. If the item was indeed mis-keyed, inappropriate decisions could be made on the basis of the test results, and particularly with "high-stakes" tests, the consequences could be serious.

There is a second ethical problem raised by this case. It was the responsibility of the psychologist using the test to assure its appropriateness to the assessment task at hand. Knowing that the test contained a mis-keyed item and continuing to use the test raised ethical problems in themselves. In choosing to continue using the test, the consulting psychologist should have assured that the scoring adjustment actually accomplished its intended purpose and preserved the integrity of the results. The psychologist discovering the error might have found another test to use to measure the same construct. In the event there was no acceptable alternative measure, the validity of an alternative scoring system would need to have been considered. Simply counting the questionably scored item correct, while probably not likely to do much harm, was a procedure that had not been empirically examined for its effects on validity.

Finally, although the psychologist who discovered the mis-keyed item did try in good faith to bring the problem to the attention of the test publisher, he might have been a bit more assertive about the problem when he received a hostile response and then was subsequently ignored.

Taking the matter to a higher level of the organization or bringing the matter to an ethics review panel might also have been appropriate.

D. Case Implications

Psychologists employed by test publishers need to be alert to ways of upgrading the delivery of psychological services. They should seek to change company policies which might impair the quality of the products affecting the welfare of test takers. Publishers of tests need to develop procedures that encourage possible problems with a measure to be brought to the attention of appropriate persons in the firm.

In addition, persons encountering such unethical behavior by psychologists should be encouraged to file formal ethical complaints when a resolution of the situation cannot be achieved through direct contact. This will help to assure that the ethically problematic behavior does not go unaddressed.

Case 6 _____

Personnel Screening for
Emotional Stability

A. *Statement of the Problem*

An I/O psychologist employed by a state civil service agency received a
request from the state correctional agency to develop a psychological
screening procedure for use as part of the process of selecting correctional
officers. The assessment procedures were to be used to weed out persons
emotionally unfit for this high-stress, emotionally demanding job. The I/O
psychologist began work on the assignment by conducting a review of the
research literature on personality assessment in employment settings (including correctional jobs) and by reading test reviews. The psychologist
discussed the proposed screening program with 10 psychologists located
throughout the country. These psychologists were knowledgeable about
the appropriate assessment of personnel in high-risk jobs such as correctional officers, police officers, and nuclear power plant operators.

The I/O psychologist then conducted a job analysis; in this process a
dozen job-related, personal characteristics of correctional officers were
identified and defined. Potential rejection indicators and possible job difficulties were also described.

The objective of the psychological assessment procedures was to
screen out at the post-conditional-offer phase persons who were likely to
be unstable, dangerous, or violent. Two objective personality measures, for
which an extensive research history existed, were selected for use in the
assessment process. In addition, evidence from background investigations
and oral examinations was included among the selection components.

The I/O psychologist retained the services of some clinical psychologists who were skilled in assessing some of the particular behavioral difficulties for which the selection program was intended to screen. However,
the clinicians were not trained in the principles or legal requirements of
personnel selection, nor were they familiar with the correctional officer
jobs. Before the post-conditional-offer emotional stability screening process
began, the I/O psychologist thoroughly oriented the clinical psychologists
in the general strategy to be used in screening candidates, the results of
the job analysis, the requirement that all assessments made must be job
related, and the established policy that no applicant would be screened

out solely on the basis of scores on the personality measures. The clinical psychologists played a key role in reviewing the personality profiles and the evidence of desirable and undesirable applicant behaviors from the background investigations and oral examinations. They also determined the need to conduct additional assessments before recommending the elimination of an applicant from the selection process. The I/O psychologist reviewed all completed assessments to ensure they were job related and consistent with good selection practice.

B. Ethics Code Standards

Ethical Standard 1.04   Boundaries of Competence

(a) Psychologists provide services . . . only within the boundaries of their competence, based on their education, training, supervised experience, or appropriate professional experience. (b) Psychologists provide services . . . in new areas or involving new techniques only after first undertaking appropriate study, training, supervision, and/or consultation from persons who are competent in those areas or techniques.

Ethical Standard 1.05   Maintaining Expertise

Psychologists who engage in assessment, . . . organizational consulting, or other professional activities maintain a reasonable level of awareness of current scientific and professional information in their fields of activity, and undertake ongoing efforts to maintain competence in the skills they use.

Ethical Standard 1.10   Nondiscrimination

In their work-related activities, psychologists do not engage in unfair discrimination based on age, gender, race, ethnicity, national origin, religion, sexual orientation, disability, socioeconomic status, or any basis proscribed by law.

Ethical Standard 1.20   Consultations and Referrals

(b) When indicated and professionally appropriate, psychologists cooperate with other professionals in order to serve their . . . clients effectively and appropriately.

Ethical Standard 2.02   Competence and Appropriate Use of Assessments and Interventions

(a) Psychologists who develop, administer, score, interpret, or use psychological assessment techniques, interviews, tests, or instruments do so in a manner and for purposes that are appropriate in light of the research on or evidence of the usefulness and proper application of the techniques.

C. Case Interpretation

This is an example of good, rather than bad, ethical practice. The primary ethical issue in this case concerned a psychologist's being aware of the boundaries of competence and needing to obtain the aid of other professionals when a situation requires skills which the psychologist does not possess. In this case, the I/O psychologist recognized the need for the advice and counsel of psychologists with greater experience in screening for high-risk jobs. Further, the I/O psychologist recognized that personally conducting clinically oriented assessments was not within her skill set.

Clinical assessments of the type described in the case typically do not have strong, formal underpinnings of validation studies, due to the often subtle and subjective nature of the phenomena being assessed. This creates potential legal exposure for a selection program. For this reason, it is especially important to review the job relatedness and legal defensibility of the assessments, as the I/O psychologist in this case did. Assessments may have adverse impact on protected groups such as minorities, women, and older candidates. In some locations, the use of clinical instruments in personnel selection may also raise invasion of privacy issues. There were also important issues to resolve about the applicability of the Americans with Disabilities Act to this type of screening, including whether the screening constituted a medical examination and so could only be administered after a conditional offer of employment had otherwise been made. Part of practicing within one's area of competence is an obligation to remain up-to-date on ongoing changes in professional practice or the law that may have important effects on the way psychological services are executed.

The I/O psychologist in this case took several steps to ensure that the highest levels of professional standards would be met, by securing advice and assistance from other psychologists in those areas in which the I/O psychologist needed additional consultation or where the project required skills clearly outside her area of competence. Assessing the kinds of personality characteristics described in the case requires training that is not typically part of the education of most I/O psychologists. Additionally, the I/O psychologist was careful to retain oversight and professional responsibility in those areas that would normally be outside the area of competence of clinically trained psychologists, such as job analysis, maintaining job relatedness, compliance with employment-related law, and general issues of personnel selection. As the psychologist in charge, the I/O psychologist had a responsibility not only for remaining within her area of professional competence, but for ensuring that the other psychologists involved on the project did likewise.

D. Case Implications

Increasingly, the boundaries between areas of specialty blur as complex problems require multiple skill sets. It is not difficult, especially when a psychologist is trying to expand skills, inadvertently to practice outside one's area of competence. Psychologists need always to be alert to this possibility and to obtain the services of other psychologists or other professionals when projects require expertise beyond their competencies. Not only does this practice help protect against ethical violations but also synergistic effects can result from the successful creation of interdisciplinary teams.

Case 7 _____

A Spiritual Matter

A. *Statement of the Problem*

A psychologist was asked to assess several candidates for the position of director of religious education for a Catholic school. The successful candidate was to have full responsibility for administering all religious education programs and for teaching a few classes in religion. The psychologist analyzed the position's task requirements and developed a comprehensive assessment system that included measures of administrative skills, teaching ability, and knowledge of Catholicism. The psychologist assessed the first candidate and submitted a report on the candidate to the school principal, who had contracted for the assessments.

Upon receiving the report, the principal called the psychologist to say that her report was extremely thorough except that it did not mention the candidate's religious beliefs or church affiliation. The psychologist replied that the candidate's religious affiliation would be a personal matter and should not be a job requirement. The psychologist also argued that basing selection decisions on religious affiliation might be illegal under Title VII of the Civil Rights Act.

The principal disagreed with the psychologist and argued rather persuasively that parents who send their children to a Catholic school expect them to be exposed to a specific set of values and that the director of religious education would have a very difficult time instilling these values in children and teachers if he or she did not live by them. The principal also noted that certain positions in religious organizations, he was certain, were exempt from Title VII of the Civil Rights Act.

The psychologist, without further exploration or consultation, found the principal's arguments persuasive and recalled vaguely that there probably was a Title VII exemption for religious organizations. The psychologist agreed to revise the assessment process and gathered the requested religious information for the first candidate and for all of the remaining candidates. The psychologist noted that candidates who were not reported to be Catholic were not interviewed by the principal.

B. *Ethics Code Standards*

Ethical Standard 1.04   Boundaries of Competence

(a) Psychologists provide services . . . only within the bound-

aries of their competence, based on their education, training, supervised experience, or appropriate professional experience.

Ethical Standard 1.06   Basis for Scientific and Professional Judgments

Psychologists rely on scientifically and professionally derived knowledge when making scientific or professional judgments or when engaging in scholarly or professional endeavors.

Ethical Standard 1.08   Human Differences

Where differences of age, gender, race, ethnicity, national origin, religion, sexual orientation, disability, language, or socioeconomic status significantly affect psychologists' work concerning particular individuals or groups, psychologists obtain the training, experience, consultation, or supervision necessary to ensure the competence of their services, or they make appropriate referrals.

Ethical Standard 1.10   Nondiscrimination

In their work-related activities, psychologists do not engage in unfair discrimination based on age, gender, race, ethnicity, national origin, religion, sexual orientation, disability, socioeconomic status, or any basis proscribed by law.

Ethical Standard 1.14   Avoiding Harm

Psychologists take reasonable steps to avoid harming their . . . clients . . . and others with whom they work, and to minimize harm where it is foreseeable and unavoidable.

C. Case Interpretation

Although the psychologist in this case may not have been guilty of an ethical violation, her performance and application of ethical standards were questionable for several reasons. First, given the circumstances of the assessment, the psychologist should have anticipated and explored, in advance of the assessment, issues of religious affiliation that predictably would be raised under these circumstances. Second, when the issues of religious affiliation did come to the forefront, the psychologist was entirely too casual in responding to them without a factual basis.

Certainly the psychologist should have taken the concerns of the principal seriously. However, in the absence of relevant knowledge, she should have delayed a decision on the matter until definitive sources of information had been consulted and the basis for a defensible position established. Even if religious inquiry were proved to be legal, alternatives to making job candidacy contingent on a particular religious affiliation might have been explored. Perhaps it would have been possible, for example, to assess whether a candidate would be able to instill the appropriate values in children without having to determine religious affiliation.

Overall, the psychologist should have realized that this was not a routine assessment concern and that the issues raised were complex and potentially far-reaching. As reported, the psychologist may not have been competent on the basis of her own knowledge to handle the relevant legal issues and probably should have consulted, or had her client consult, legal counsel. For instance, aside from Title VII of the Civil Rights Act, there may have been other legal factors such as state and case law to consider before making a decision about how to proceed.

D. Case Implications

Special circumstances or exceptions to the usual rules call for special and careful handling. Personal judgments need to be carefully differentiated from scientific ones. When, in new or ambiguous areas, it is necessary to take risks, it should be with the client's full understanding of the nature of those risks and the potential costs and benefits of alternative courses of action. Psychologists confronted with such complexities also need to consult with persons who have expertise other than their own when they encounter circumstances that go beyond their own competencies.

Case 8 _____

Misleading Reporting of Results

A. *Statement of the Problem*

An I/O psychologist working for a psychological consulting firm had prepared a number of test validation reports for clients. These validation reports were submitted to an examining board when the psychologist wished to become credentialed as an American Board of Professional Psychology (ABPP) diplomate.

In the validity reports prepared by the psychologist, there were typically large discrepancies between the technical reports, which averaged about 200 pages in length, and the executive summaries, which ranged from 2 to 3 pages. For example, in one case, the executive summary suggested that 85 job incumbents were involved in the research sample. However, the actual statistical analyses described in the technical report were based on only 26 job incumbents, although the original plan had been to test 85. Additionally, the summary referred to the "high degree of validity" that was obtained; in fact, the validity coefficient cited in the larger report was only .11. The ABPP examiners rejected the applicant's candidacy.

B. *Ethics Code Standards*

Ethical Standard 1.14   Avoiding Harm

Psychologists take reasonable steps to avoid harming their . . . clients, research participants, students, and others with whom they work, and to minimize harm where it is foreseeable and unavoidable.

Ethical Standard 1.23   Documentation of Professional and Scientific Work

(a) Psychologists appropriately document their professional and scientific work in order to facilitate provision of services later by them or by other professionals, to ensure accountability, and to meet other requirements of institutions or the law.

The psychologist would also have benefited from being familiar with the requirements of the SIOP's *Principles for the Validation and Use of Personnel Selection Procedures* (SIOP, 1987). These *Principles* encourage full disclosure and avoidance of misrepresentation of data.

C. Case Interpretation

The best interests of the client are not served by the preparation of report summaries which misrepresent the soundness of the test validation research supporting an assessment procedure. Such misrepresentations contribute to the potential misuse of the results and interpretations of the assessments and potentially cause harm to the client.

Because the psychologist knew the limitations of the study (such as small sample sizes and the very low validity coefficients of the tests), it was ethically inappropriate to misrepresent the findings. Certainly the clients should have been unambiguously informed of the actual results of the validity studies and of any limitations on using the tests in practice. The possible harm to the client and to applicants exposed to the procedure was foreseeable and could and should have been avoided.

By claiming a high degree of validity when there was very limited validity evidence, and by reporting planned as opposed to actual sample size in the summaries, the psychologist made seemingly fraudulent and at the least misleading statements. Reservations regarding the validation results of the assessment procedure were not acknowledged when, in fact, there were many.

The psychologist also should have been familiar with the SIOP *Principles* cited above. Among other provisions, these *Principles* in this case suggest that samples employed in validity studies be described sufficiently for the reader to judge their pertinence to the client's practical application of these results. Furthermore, the psychologist seemingly ignored the requirements of SIOP's *Principles* (SIOP, 1987, pp. 31–32) that (a) reports not be misleading, (b) research findings which might qualify the conclusions be reported, and (c) the impression not be given that an assessment program is more useful than it really is.

Specific to the facts of this case, the executive summary should have reported the actual sample size as opposed to the planned research sample and explained that with a sample of that size, the results of the research, which were quite unimpressive from a predictive validity standpoint, had inherent limitations on generalizability. It would then be up to the client to decide whether to take the risk involved in using the instrument.

D. Case Implications

Whether by design or through negligence, inaccurate reporting of research findings can mislead those who, in good faith, make use of the results of test validation procedures. Since inappropriate use of assessment techniques can have severe consequences in altering the lives of test takers and cost organizational clients considerable time, effort, and money, psychologists must use care in assuring that their validation studies are accurately represented.

Executive summaries should accurately represent and communicate the nature of the validity evidence. This is especially important in reports directed to a managerial audience, since they are often key decision makers and may not have available to them staff psychologists or other persons technically competent to interpret the results. The psychologist has to make sure that the decision makers understand all of the pros and cons of using a test with whatever limitations it has. Psychologists must also have adequate knowledge of psychological measurement principles to interpret their research findings correctly in light of the actual circumstances of their studies.

Case 9 _____

"Realistic Job Previews" and the Selection of Female Employees

A. *Statement of the Problem*

A psychologist employed by a consulting firm was retained by a company to design a selection procedure for a job that had traditionally been filled by males. The manager for the company acknowledged that the company had experienced significant problems with the few women who had expressed interest and been placed in this job and stated that he wanted the selection procedure to include a realistic job preview. The purpose of this preview was to accentuate the physical difficulties and unpleasantries of the work so that those who did pursue it would not prematurely quit the position. The manager emphasized the costs to the company of this turnover and stressed that it was not for him an issue of keeping women out of this job, just that statistically, as a group, women had not worked out.

The psychologist agreed to assist with the project and helped to script and produce a videotape to be shown as an early step in the selection process. Although the psychologist attempted to portray a somewhat balanced picture of the job, heavy editing by the company manager and his colleagues resulted in a film that exaggerated the features of the job likely to alienate female applicants.

The film began with a statement of the company's equal employment policy and encouraged qualified candidates to apply for the job. However, the visual message contradicted the verbal message. For example, the film contained brief interviews with people who were unable to complete training, as well as those who completed training. Both of the training failures were female, while all three of the training successes were male. The film also showed men performing manual labor which appeared to require high levels of upper body strength, yet no mention was made that these activities were done only once or twice a month and that mechanical devices were available when assistance was needed. The film's few portrayals of females performing the job showed women with exhausted, frustrated expressions in unpleasant surroundings such as heavy traffic and icy weather.

At least partly because of the videotape, the number of female applicants dropped significantly. Turnover in the job also declined.

B. Ethics Code Standards

Ethical Standard 1.10   Nondiscrimination

In their work-related activities, psychologists do not engage in unfair discrimination based on age, gender, race, ethnicity, national origin, religion, sexual orientation, disability, socio-economic status, or any basis proscribed by law.

Ethical Standard 1.14   Avoiding Harm

Psychologists take reasonable steps to avoid harming their . . . clients, research participants, . . . and others with whom they work, and to minimize harm where it is foreseeable and unavoidable.

Ethical Standard 1.16   Misuse of Psychologists' Work

(a) Psychologists do not participate in activities in which it appears likely that their skills or data will be misused by others, unless corrective mechanisms are available.

C. Case Interpretation

The presentation of material describing the negative features of a job is appropriate as long as the material is accurate, representative, and not directed adversely or preferentially toward a particular group. In this case, it is reasonable to conclude that the job preview was intended to be used to deter women from applying for the job. The film portrayed the job unrealistically and was slanted toward isolated aspects of the job likely to be offensive to female applicants. The film resulted in fewer women applying for the job than the already low rate in place prior to the implementation of the film in the selection procedure.

In addition, there were moral and legal issues involved in this case since the potential net result of the procedure was to affect the adverse impact statistics at all stages of the selection process by increasing the number of women who voluntarily opted out of the selection process at an early stage. If the preview had portrayed physically demanding work realistically, the results, though possibly the same, might have been interpreted in a different light. Because the videotape specifically targeted females, the preview and the selection procedure were no longer face neutral.

Concerning the psychologist's specific role in this case, the matter is complicated. On the surface, the psychologist was not personally responsible for the development of the offensive and final version of the videotape. The changes were made after his involvement with the project. The ethicality of his behavior might on that basis not be questioned. Still, he should have realized that there was a considerable potential for abuse and misuse of his efforts in this case and have taken reasonable steps to assure that his services were not misdirected. At the least, if he were to be involved at all, he should have insisted that he be involved throughout the project and have had the opportunity to review the final product before its release.

D. Case Implications

In considering whether a procedure to be used in conjunction with selection efforts is appropriate, psychologists should consider the procedure in its total context. Sensitivity is needed as to how the various components of a selection procedure might affect individual applicants and specific groups of applicants. When a psychologist is asked to target a particular group as part of a selection process, it should be determined by the psychologist whether the targeting is in violation of ethical standards or potentially at odds with relevant laws. Of course, judgment will be needed, and at times all relevant facts or intentions may not be available. Omniscience is neither required nor expected. However, when an initially appropriate behavior turns out to have been problematic, the prudent course of action is to make appropriate corrections to minimize harm.

Psychologists also need to be aware of potential conflicts that may arise between the desires of organizational managers; federal, state, or local laws; and the psychologists' own ethical responsibilities. If a psychologist feels that the selection tool or process asked to be developed is or might be in violation of the ethical or legal guidelines or likely will be misused, then the issues need to be resolved to the psychologist's satisfaction before making a decision to proceed with the assignment.

Case 10 _____

Developing International
Selection Systems

A. Statement of the Problem

A multinational electronics firm was using a selection system for midlevel managers in the United States and wanted to adapt the procedure to select midlevel managers in France. The firm asked an I/O psychologist in the United States if she would be interested in helping to modify the system for use in France. The psychologist indicated that she presently was not acquainted with French selection practices but that she was interested in the assignment and would take the necessary steps to modify the system appropriately.

Working with the company's French-speaking staff, the psychologist began the project by conducting a job analysis of the midlevel manager position in the French organization. Based on the results of the job analysis, she made some substantive changes to the U.S. version of the selection system. She then had the entire selection instrument translated into French and back-translated into English to confirm the fidelity of the translation. The back-translation revealed a few minor content and stylistic issues, which were modified in the final translated version. The psychologist then conducted item analyses and a concurrent validation study with 112 midlevel managers throughout the French operation.

When completed, the study generated statistically significant results, but a few of the managers who completed the instrument complained that they had not received feedback on their results. The psychologist was asked to develop an interpretive feedback, which could be used to summarize each individual participant's results. The psychologist indicated that the instrument was essentially the same as the version used in the United States and that the measure generated only raw scores and percentile scores. The psychologist further stated that developmental feedback would be unnecessary once the procedure was implemented because the instrument would only be used for selecting job applicants.

Continuing with the selection aspects of the work, the psychologist made some minor changes to the instrument based on the validation study and implemented the procedure to select all midlevel managers as specified in the original contract. After a few weeks into the project, however, the psychologist received a call from her contact in the client organization, who expressed some serious concerns about the selection system in the French location. A number of applicants who completed the selection procedure had requested feedback on their results and were disturbed by the lack of information they received in response. They did not find the score and normative data to be of much assistance to them. In addition, the test administrators were unhappy with the selection system because they felt, consistent with their customary practices, that it was the company's responsibility to offer applicants, successful or not, the opportunity to receive feedback in a face-to-face meeting. The client's representatives indicated that they agreed with the test administrators and would have to discontinue using the selecting system until it included interpretive feedback procedures they found acceptable.

B. Ethics Code Standards

Ethical Standard 1.08   Human Differences

Where differences of ... national origin ... [or] language ... significantly affect psychologists' work concerning particular individuals or groups, psychologists obtain the training, experience, consultation, or supervision necessary to ensure the competence of their services, or they make appropriate referrals.

Ethical Standard 2.04   Use of Assessment in General and With Special Populations

(c) Psychologists attempt to identify situations in which particular interventions or assessment techniques ... may require adjustment in administration or interpretation because of factors such as ... ethnicity, national origin, ... [or] language. ...

Ethical Standard 2.09   Explaining Assessment Results

Unless the nature of the relationship is clearly explained to the person being assessed in advance and precludes provision of an explanation of results (such as in some organizational consulting, preemployment or security screenings, and forensic evaluations), psychologists ensure that an explanation of the results is provided using language that is reasonably understandable to the person assessed. ...

C. Case Interpretation

This case highlights the psychologist's responsibility to be sensitive to cultural differences. The psychologist appears to have behaved competently and ethically from a psychometric perspective. The job analysis, translation, back-translation, item analyses, and local validation were apparently performed in a manner consistent with professional standards. However, the psychologist was not sensitive to the fact that aside from test content there are many other cultural differences with respect to psychological testing that a psychologist working in a different culture may need to take into account.

Rather than awaiting issues to be brought to her attention, the psychologist should have been more proactive in exploring nonlanguage cultural differences between the two countries. For instance, the psychologist might have consulted with psychologists and other relevant professionals in France. Equally troublesome, the psychologist actually dismissed client feedback that had highlighted a distinction between how the psychologist viewed feedback practices in the United States and France. Not atypically for French companies, or for European organizations more generally, the client company focused less on the psychometric aspects of the selection than is typical for U.S. companies. Conversely, there was a strong concern, mostly ignored by the psychologist, about the effects of the new selection system on applicants. It was the custom with this company to offer applicants and employees the opportunity to receive extensive interpretive feedback when asked to complete a psychological test. The psychologist erred by essentially ignoring the request to modify the method and by ignoring the importance to the company's officials of certain values which may not have been held by organizations with whom the psychologist had worked in her parent country.

Certainly, if the originally contracted budget did not contain sufficient funds for providing the additional feedback, some modification of the contract price might have been needed. However, simply to ignore the request was neither ethically nor practically appropriate.

D. Case Implications

Psychologists need to recognize that the appropriate professional practices and client concerns may vary across cultures. Psychologists of course have no ethical obligation to work in such cultures, but when they do accept or seek out such projects, they have an ethical responsibility to take account of, and respond to, alternative cultural expectations. Whenever it is possible and not ethically or technically inappropriate to do so, psychologists should take the necessary steps to assure that they have modified their products or services to take account of expectations and needs to which they are not necessarily accustomed.

Case 11

Assessment Center Records

A. Statement of the Problem

A psychologist working as an internal consultant was responsible for the development and ongoing oversight of a well-regarded assessment program for evaluating and developing middle managers. From the start of the program, the psychologist was very conscientious about archiving all the information that was generated by the program, including the assessors' notes.

One important aspect of the training program involved critiquing raters' observations to help them develop their skills as assessors. Occasionally, new assessors recorded inappropriate written comments (rather idiosyncratic personal observations or opinions which might, if taken out of context, be misunderstood). Such remarks were typically brought to the assessors' attention by the supervising psychologist and were corrected in the final record for each affected assessee. All versions of the assessors' notes were retained, however, in the interests of having a complete record and in order to document training needs and the progress made by new assessors. The notes were retained on the original forms, which identified by name the persons who were being commented upon.

A suit was subsequently initiated on behalf of a protected group member complaining of racial discrimination in the selection procedures. A class of affected persons was certified because of the disproportionately small number of similar group members in the target management job. Following an exhaustive discovery process, in which all records were subpoenaed and obtained, a significant issue was made in the litigation about the inappropriate comments found in the files that had been written by a few of the new assessors. Partly as a result of these remarks, the company agreed to a substantial settlement, including discontinuance of the assessment program.

B. Ethics Code Standards

Ethical Standard 1.14   Avoiding Harm

Psychologists take reasonable steps to avoid harming their

... clients ... and others with whom they work, and to minimize harm where it is foreseeable and unavoidable.

Ethical Standard 1.23   Documentation of Professional and Scientific Work

(a) Psychologists appropriately document their professional and scientific work in order to facilitate provision of services later by them or by other professionals, to ensure accountability, and to meet other requirements of institutions or the law.

Ethical Standard 5.04   Maintenance of Records

Psychologists maintain appropriate confidentiality in creating, storing, accessing, transferring, and disposing of records under their control, whether these are written, automated, or in any other medium. Psychologists maintain and dispose of records in accordance with law and in a manner that permits compliance with the requirements of this Ethics Code.

Ethical Standard 5.10   Ownership of Records and Data

Recognizing that ownership of records and data is governed by legal principles, psychologists take reasonable and lawful steps so that records and data remain available to the extent needed to serve the best interests of ... organizational clients ... or appropriate others.

C. Case Interpretation

In this case, a problem resulted from the recording and storing of too much rather than too little information. In most applied settings it is generally safe to assume that any information recorded in a written format has the potential later to be used in legal actions against a client organization. Of course, records must be complete and accurate. Potentially misleading or negatively interpreted information about an individual may certainly be recorded so long as it is accurate and defensible. Care must always be taken to balance the goals of technical accuracy and thoroughness and minimizing the risk of later misuse of recorded notes.

In this case, the inappropriate remarks were intended to be used solely for purposes of training assessors. In fact, they resulted in a potentially damaging, entirely unintended, use by others who may have had less than benevolent motivations. The psychologist should have more carefully considered not just the need to document the ongoing activities of an assessment but also the risk to the organizational client of having this type of information in a version that could later adversely impact the client in any legal proceeding.

In today's highly litigious climate, it is worse than ethically naive not to consider that all recorded information might later be used in adversarial legal proceedings. Were it desirable to document observations for purposes of training, particularly when the recorded remarks might not rise to a professional standard of practice, those records might have been clearly separated from official ones and destroyed at the end of their training purposes.

D. Case Implications

Ethical mandates must be balanced against practical realities and threats they might cause to clients' well-being. In the abstract, full and complete documentation of research is a strong professional and ethical requirement that is appropriately emphasized in graduate and professional training. Accurately recorded information might prove useful in documenting assessment decisions, but also in providing feedback to individual assessees. However, excessively detailed documentation may in some instances be unnecessary and possibly even be inimical both to the best interests of the organizational client and to the individual assessees, particularly when false, misleading, or tangential remarks are recorded. Organizational psychologists must consider all possible uses as well as potential abuses of data collected before determining how best to document their work.

Case 12

Maintaining Confidentiality and Objectivity

A. Statement of the Problem

A multinational organization contracted with a consulting psychologist to assess candidates for promotion to an executive-level job in a socially conservative country. The psychologist was a male in his mid-thirties. The psychologist conducted the assessments and recommended a male candidate who had a stellar performance record with the company and showed the most potential for the new job. The recommended candidate was also highly regarded by top management. The individual selected was scheduled to begin the new job after a 2-week vacation.

Before leaving on vacation, the new executive, who had always been friendly with the psychologist, met with him and expressed relief over the results of the assessment. The executive then started rambling a bit in idle conversation. His expression appeared to be worried. Sensing there might be something troubling the executive, the psychologist asked if there were other issues on his mind. The executive then confided growing anxieties over some unelaborated personal conflicts and revealed that the real purpose of his 2-week "vacation" was to seek out some professional counseling. The executive stated that he was particularly eager to resolve the conflicts before starting his new job. He noted that top management knew nothing about this issue and believed the executive really was indeed taking a vacation prior to going overseas.

The psychologist expressed empathy, suggested (upon request) the name of a good clinical psychologist, and agreed to keep the foregoing discussion confidential. The executive thanked the psychologist for his understanding and advice.

When leaving, the executive hugged and, to the psychologist's surprise and embarrassment, quickly but not too subtly, fondled the psychologist. The psychologist chose to ignore the gesture and bade the executive a polite farewell.

After some reflection on the matter, the psychologist decided not to say anything to top management about the meeting, including the behavior that occurred at the close of the meeting. He felt bound by his promise to keep the conversation confidential. The psychologist concluded that the executive deserved an opportunity to perform well in the new job. He believed that whatever problems might arise in the new job could be satisfactorily dealt with at that time by the company and the executive.

B. Ethics Code Standards

Ethical Standard 1.03   Professional and Scientific Relationship

Psychologists provide diagnostic, therapeutic, teaching, research, supervisory, consultative, or other psychological services only in the context of a defined professional or scientific relationship or role.

Ethical Standard 1.04   Boundaries of Competence

(a) Psychologists provide services . . . only within the boundaries of their competence, based on their education, training, supervised experience, or appropriate professional experience.

Ethical Standard 1.10   Nondiscrimination

In their work-related activities, psychologists do not engage in unfair discrimination based on . . . sexual orientation. . . .

Ethical Standard 1.21   Third-Party Requests for Services

(a) When a psychologist agrees to provide services to a person or entity at the request of a third party, the psychologist clarifies to the extent feasible, at the outset of the service, the nature of the relationship with each party. This clarification includes the role of the psychologist . . . , the probable uses of the services provided or the information obtained, and the fact that there may be limits to the confidentiality.

Ethical Standard 5.01   Discussing the Limits of Confidentiality

(a) Psychologists discuss with persons and organizations with whom they establish a scientific or professional relationship . . . (1) the relevant limitations on confidentiality . . . in organizational consulting, and (2) the foreseeable uses of the information generated through their services.

Ethical Standard 5.02   Maintaining Confidentiality

Psychologists have a primary obligation and take reasonable precautions to respect the confidentiality rights of those with whom they work or consult. . . .

C. Case Interpretation

The psychologist did not necessarily behave unethically in the delicate and complicated issues raised by this case. Perhaps, since a client relationship had not been defined with the executive, the psychologist might have been better advised not to have given the executive the opportunity to continue the discussion beyond the opening pleasantries. When it became clear that the individual had some possibly serious psychological concerns to discuss, immediate clarification of the psychologist's role and the confidentiality assumptions would have been appropriate.

Nevertheless, the psychologist properly did not permit the remaining discussion to become a counseling session, which the psychologist was untrained to conduct. Although the psychologist was appropriately puzzled by the fondling behavior, and the issues it might potentially raise concerning the overseas assignment, the decision not to bring it to management's attention was probably acceptable. It is open to discussion whether the fondling was covered by the psychologist's promise to keep the prior conversation confidential, although the psychologist possibly communicated the impression that the entire interaction was to be considered confidential. Indeed, the assurances of confidentiality in a situation in which confidentiality was not legally protected created potential conflicts for all parties. In this case, the executive's behavior appeared not to pose a serious threat to anyone at the time it occurred, and it is quite possible that the executive would refrain from engaging in such behavior in his new job. However, the psychologist might have brought to the executive's attention the inappropriateness of his behavior.

D. Case Implications

I/O psychologists involved in assessments may through casual contact or otherwise learn of many aspects of the behavior or character of persons being assessed. They need to be cautious and to use good judgment in defining client–consultant roles and in any promises of confidentiality they make. In the industrial context, obtained information or assurances of confidentiality may lead to unexpected complications. Psychologists need to identify and to anticipate occasions where there may be legal or case-specific limitations to the confidentiality the psychologist can or should exercise. They also need to be sensitive to and guard against any personal biases they might have, such as, for example, attitudes toward sexual orientation, that could influence their professional judgments.

Case 13 _____

The Right Not to Participate in Selection Activities

A. *Statement of the Problem*

An I/O psychologist specializing in measurement issues in personnel selection was interested in evaluating the effectiveness of a newly developed biodata questionnaire for predicting customer service ability. After contacting a number of organizations about completing a research project using their current employees, the I/O psychologist received a positive response from the HR manager of a local sporting goods company.

The HR manager said that the company had been experiencing low sales volume, high levels of shrinkage, and low customer satisfaction ratings. The president of the company had asked the HR department on several occasions to investigate selection systems that could screen out applicants who were likely to be poor performers. In a meeting with the manager and the company president, the I/O psychologist presented a proposal for evaluating the biodata questionnaire and for possibly using the research results in future selection efforts at the company.

In his proposal, the I/O psychologist described the potential benefits of a tailored selection procedure for improving organizational performance. The company president was enthusiastic about the proposal, particularly so since it would not cost him anything, and directed the HR manager to begin work on the project immediately.

The I/O psychologist provided the HR manager with packets of biodata questionnaires and performance appraisal forms for all employees, with the instructions to store managers to administer the questionnaires during a 2-week period. During the first week of administration, the HR manager received phone calls from numerous store managers asking what to do with employees who refused to complete the questionnaire. The employees were reportedly uncomfortable with the personal nature of some of the questions and were skeptical about how their answers would be used by the company.

The HR manager presented the problem to the company's president, who was suspicious of the employees' unwillingness to respond to the questionnaire. He felt that if the employees had nothing to hide, they would have no problems answering the questions candidly. He instructed the HR manager to send a fax to all store managers saying that completion of the questionnaire was a condition of employment and that refusal by any employee could result in termination.

The HR manager also sent a copy of the fax to the I/O psychologist, who immediately requested a meeting with the company president. The I/O psychologist asked that the manager send a fax to the store managers, explaining that participation in the project was voluntary for all employees. It suggested that the store managers direct concerned employees to the I/O psychologist, who could answer questions about the project and respond to any fears or other concerns. The I/O psychologist received phone calls from 11 employees, and after he talked with them about the research process, all but 3 of the employees agreed to participate.

B. Ethics Code Standards

Ethical Standard 6.07   Responsibility

(b) Psychologists are responsible for the ethical conduct of research conducted by them or by others under their supervision or control.

Ethical Standard 6.11   Informed Consent to Research

(a) Psychologists use language that is reasonably understandable to research participants in obtaining their appropriate informed consent. . . . Such informed consent is appropriately documented.

(b) Using language that is reasonably understandable to participants, psychologists inform participants of the nature of the research; they inform participants that they are free to participate or to decline to participate or to withdraw from the research; they explain the foreseeable consequences of declining or withdrawing; they inform participants of significant factors that may be expected to influence their willingness to participate (such as risks, discomfort, adverse effects, or limitations on confidentiality . . .); and they explain other aspects about which the prospective participants inquire.

(c) When psychologists conduct research with individuals such as . . . subordinates, [they] take special care to protect the prospective participants from adverse consequences of declining or withdrawing from participation.

C. Case Interpretation

This case concerns the responsibility of I/O psychologists in conducting research and professional practice to protect the rights of participants and of nonparticipants, especially the right not to participate in a study or intervention project. The psychologist in this case appropriately and forcefully acted to correct inappropriate pressure being put on respondents for participation as soon as he learned of it. There is no indication that anyone actually complied with the chief executive officer's edict, and so, presumably, there was no immediate damage.

Still, the psychologist could and should have done more at the outset of the project to assure that the terms of participation and the opportunity to participate or not (informed consent) were adequately communicated. Those sponsoring the research should have known the nature of the project, that participation was voluntary, and that pressure would not be put on potential participants to complete the form against their wishes. The I/O psychologist had the ethical responsibility to create conditions in which the right not to participate was clearly identified and in which those who did participate did so on the basis of informed consent.

Explicit instructions should have been given to the company president and the HR manager about the terms and conditions of the research project. In addition, written instructions (preferably, under these circumstances, including the name and phone number of the responsible I/O psychologist) should have been provided to all employees prior to administration of the questionnaires. This would have helped to ensure that all employees were free to make informed choices about participation in this research project.

D. Case Implications

I/O psychologists conducting applied research must expect that there will be many pressures upon employees to participate in research studies or interventions. When the research is sponsored by an academic researcher, the university's or college's institutional review process may help to assure protection of human participants, even those whose data are collected outside the parent institution. When research is conducted in applied settings, such as in industry, a greater burden may fall on the sponsoring psychologist to assure protection of participants and nonparticipants and to assure that informed-consent requirements have been met.

The psychologist conducting research in an employment setting may find organizational decisions and policies and implicit assumptions to be in conflict with ethical mandates. Making involvement in a research project a condition of employment provides just one and rather obvious example of how participation in psychological activities may be less than voluntary. It is true that organizations benefit from the results of applied research which have complete or near-complete samples. Nevertheless, involvement in psychological research or interventions in organizations should never be forced upon unwilling participants.

When conducting research or change projects in organizations, and particularly in cases in which there is no institutional review board to approve the practices in advance, I/O psychologists must take an active role in formulating policy assuring informed and voluntary consent to participate in psychological activities. It may be necessary to encourage change in or adaptation of existing organizational policies to assure conformity to psychologists' ethical standards. Preventative measures should anticipate as many possible contingencies as possible and proper measures then taken in advance to assure that employees' rights are not violated. At the same time, consent is often, and appropriately, implied in certain employment contexts, as, for example, when applicants rather than existing employees are tested.

Part II

Organizational Diagnosis and Intervention

Case 14 —————————————————————

Layoff Notifications

A. *Statement of the Problem*

Due to financial considerations, it became necessary for a *Fortune* 500 company to lay off a significant number of employees. Preliminary estimates indicated that the downsizing would affect about 800 employees with 600 of them being midlevel managers. One of the company's I/O psychologists was asked to work with the executive committee to help determine the extent of the downsizing and to consider the qualifications of managers necessary in the downsized company. The psychologist was advised that aside from prepared statements that the executive committee decided to release, all aspects of the project were to be treated as confidential.

The entire project was expected to take about 6 months, and the executive committee planned to announce within 3 months that a significant downsizing was being considered. The first phase of the project involved a number of strategic activities as well as considering the dismissal of specific employees. The last 3 months would be devoted to finalizing the list of those to be dismissed. All layoffs would be announced simultaneously at the end of the 6-month period.

During the first 3 months of this project, the psychologist was having a conversation with one of the managers that was being considered for dismissal. The psychologist and the manager were friends, and their families would occasionally get together to socialize. The manager indicated that he was considering purchasing a new home that was much larger than his current one. Although the manager seemed excited about the new home, he indicated that the mortgage would be a bit of a stretch. The psychologist listened attentively to the manager but did not say anything to the manager or follow up in any way.

B. *Ethics Code Standards*

Ethical Standard 1.14   Avoiding Harm

Psychologists take reasonable steps to avoid harming their patients or clients . . . and others with whom they work, and to minimize harm where it is foreseeable and unavoidable.

Ethical Standard 5.02   Maintaining Confidentiality

Psychologists have a primary obligation and take reasonable precautions to respect the confidentiality rights of those with whom they work or consult. . . .

Ethical Standard 5.05   Disclosures

(b) Psychologists also may disclose confidential information with the appropriate consent of the . . . organizational client. . . .

C. Case Interpretation

The psychologist did not behave unethically in this case. The information regarding the downsizing and the manager's upcoming dismissal was confidential, and the psychologist honored this condition. However, there are a number of other ways the psychologist could have handled this situation that might have been more effective in minimizing harm to the soon-to-be-laid-off manager and to other similarly affected employees.

In this case, the client was the organization's top management. Yet, there were peripheral obligations to other affected parties. Ideally, the psychologist should have recognized and attempted to address the ethical issues associated with withholding such critical information from employees for a relatively long period of time. The psychologist could have discussed these ethical issues with the executive committee at the beginning of this assignment. There are a number of practical strategies that could have been pursued that might have minimized harm to employees. Some of these possibilities raise new ethical concerns.

For example, the psychologist might have advised the manager to think carefully about purchasing the home with a general argument such as "Is that a wise decision in today's business climate?" Although this is seemingly helpful and ethical, it is probably inappropriate. This response probably does not give the manager enough information about his future, and the psychologist is coming very close to disclosing or implying the confidential information. This response also does not help any of the other employees who will also be dismissed.

An alternative response might have been to discuss the issue with the executive committee and, in accord with Ethical Standard 5.05, seek permission to inform the manager that he might be dismissed in the near future. This approach, however, also does not help the other employees who will be let go. Thus, the most appropriate response at this point might be to encourage senior management to consider more carefully how best to provide advance notification of upcoming dismissals.

D. Case Implications

Real-life organizational practice presents many dilemmas and conflicts, in which simple client–psychologist principles of confidentiality have limitations. Psychologists should recognize, in advance, that withholding information that will significantly impact employees' lives, such as whether they will be dismissed, can be harmful to them. Although there are often a variety of good reasons to avoid releasing such information immediately, there are ethical implications associated with withholding this information for a long period of time, and psychologists should be proactive in balancing the interests and needs of the employer and other affected parties.

Case 15

Survey Reveals Sexual Harassment

A. Statement of the Problem

A consulting firm conducted an anonymous employee opinion survey for a large retail organization with a number of stores. The survey results, including write-in comments, which were encouraged, were to be submitted to the HR department at the headquarters of the corporation that had engaged the consulting firm. They were to review all findings, including written comments, and had told the management of the corporation's stores that the managers would receive these findings.

Two employees in one store had written in comments saying that they were being sexually harassed. The identity of the alleged harasser was clear because there was only one manager in their particular store. The consulting firm's project director, a psychologist, took no special action and forwarded the survey results and the write-in comments to corporate headquarters and to the relevant store locations as had been planned.

B. Ethics Code Standards

> **Ethical Standard 1.14   Avoiding Harm**
>
> **Psychologists take reasonable steps to avoid harming their patients or clients . . . and others with whom they work, and to minimize harm where it is foreseeable and unavoidable.**

> **Ethical Standard 1.20   Consultations and Referrals**
>
> **(b) When indicated and professionally appropriate, psychologists cooperate with other professionals in order to serve their . . . clients effectively and appropriately.**

C. Case Interpretation

The consulting firm's psychologist did not necessarily behave unethically in this case. The appropriate course of action depended partly on the specific terms of the survey administration, any assurances made of anonymity or confidentiality, and whether the participants had been advised at the time of completing the instrument that the results, including comments, would be shared with their store manager(s).

In this case, the psychologist might have been more proactive in drawing the relevant comments to corporate management's attention. Allegations of sexual harassment are potentially significant and almost always sensitive issues; they should be addressed, not ignored. In addition, the survey feedback process needed to be managed so that the feedback regarding sexual harassment allegations did not lead to any inappropriate actions by or toward the store manager or other affected parties, including those making the assertion.

The company representatives, having learned from the survey results of the allegations, may have had a legal and/or ethical obligation to proceed with a formal investigation of the allegations of sexual harassment. By contacting the organization's corporate staff to discuss the allegations and the possible courses of action needed to address them, the psychologist could have helped to assure that the appropriate individuals in the organization were aware of the charges and had been offered assistance in creating a legally and ethically appropriate course of responsive action.

D. Case Implications

Psychologists should realize that their responsibilities concerning projects may vary depending upon the specific circumstances of the case. If psychologists unexpectedly encounter significant information that may possibly be overlooked or mishandled by others, they should accept responsibility for bringing the information to management's attention, even when this is not a formal, predetermined consulting responsibility.

Nonetheless, anonymously reported allegations of sexual harassment must be considered within the context within which the information was generated or obtained, taking due care to avoid unintended harmful consequences. Psychologists should assist companies in addressing such allegations in ways that address the company's obligations not to ignore such assertions once they have been made, but which also do not destroy survey participants' perceptions or assurances of a survey's anonymity. The possibility of defamation of character charges if harassment allegations prove unfounded must also be considered.

Case 16 _____

Implementing New Technology

A. Statement of the Problem

A company asked its recently hired I/O psychologist if computer-aided monitoring might improve the productivity of its clerical workers. Generally familiar with the technology, the psychologist replied that he thought it could help and advised that the information collected could be used to set new standards for evaluating performance and for rewarding, disciplining, or dismissing workers.

On the basis of the psychologist's recommendation, the company's management decided to initiate an employee-monitoring system. The psychologist was given primary responsibility for designing and implementing it. Although the psychologist became extremely proficient in the technical aspects of the monitoring system, he gave little consideration to the broader systemic issues that are often associated with new interventions. For instance, the psychologist did not review the literature or contact other organizations to determine how this technology might be received by employees.

The productivity of the clerical staff increased soon after the technology was implemented, but so did turnover. The psychologist learned from exit interviews with the departing employees that the new system had been very distressing to them. They also resented having the system imposed upon them without having had a say in how it would be designed and its results used. Additional interviews with some of the employees who had not left the company revealed some of the same sentiments, though they seemed to be held with less intensity.

The psychologist decided to discuss the situation in his next regularly scheduled meeting with top management and to suggest that a group of employees be consulted on the merits and potential redesign of the system. But in the next meeting with top management, the psychologist was preempted by praise and the promise from his superiors of a promotion for him. They had been very impressed with the productivity gains. They remarked that they had noticed the upswing in turnover and wondered whether it could have been at least partly triggered by the new system. Yet they expressed no real concern, saying instead that the productivity gains would more than offset the cost of replacing workers who left voluntarily. The meeting then moved to the next item on the agenda. The psychologist decided to let the matter rest, thinking that perhaps he had placed too much credence on a few disgruntled employees who might have been dismissed eventually anyway.

B. Ethics Code Standards

Ethical Standard 1.04   Boundaries of Competence

(b) Psychologists provide services . . . in new areas or involving new techniques only after first undertaking appropriate study . . . and/or consultation from persons who are competent in those areas or techniques.

Ethical Standard 1.05   Maintaining Expertise

Psychologists who engage in assessment, . . . organizational consulting, or other professional activities maintain a reasonable level of awareness of current scientific and professional information in their fields of activity, and undertake ongoing efforts to maintain competence in the skills they use.

Ethical Standard 1.15   Misuse of Psychologists' Influence

Because psychologists' scientific and professional judgments and actions may affect the lives of others, they are alert to and guard against personal, financial, social, organizational, or political factors that might lead to misuse of their influence.

C. Case Interpretation

The psychologist in this case failed to consider at the outset of the project that the technology, depending on how it was designed and used, might have a negative effect on employee attitudes and increase turnover. Although it is generally impossible to foresee all of the potential consequences of implementing new technology, it is well-established knowledge that specific interventions will often have broader implications, and the psychologist should have anticipated and prepared for this. Additionally, personal ambition was allowed to suppress the need to make management aware of the identified problems and corrective steps that might have been taken.

D. Case Implications

Before advising clients or managers about any technology, I/O psychologists have a professional responsibility to acquire knowledge about all relevant aspects of the project, particularly when it can reasonably be assumed there may be broader effects on the organization. Furthermore, alternative ways to design and use the technology and other possible interventions that might avoid or minimize negative effects should always be considered before deciding on a particular course of intervention. Finally, psychologists need to recognize the ways in which their own personal ambitions and needs can influence their recommendations and be careful to consider how they may adversely affect their work with clients.

Confidential Feedback Using Electronic Mail

A. Statement of the Problem

A psychologist employed as an internal consultant for a large, decentralized organization was responsible for implementing a 360° feedback process for a large segment of the organization. In this technique, managers or other employees receive feedback from a variety of sources in the organization, including subordinates, peers, and superiors. Typically, as in this case, the data may be anonymously or at least confidentially collected, and the feedback does not report the identities of evaluators except by group (subordinates, supervisors, etc.).

In the search for a cost-effective solution to this assignment, the psychologist contracted with the firm's management information system (MIS) department to implement the feedback program using the company's existing electronic mail (E-mail) system. Questionnaires were "distributed" using E-mail, and employees were able to respond on their terminals with assurances of anonymity. The system was implemented with great enthusiasm, and the psychologist was given special recognition for her cost-saving idea.

When the psychologist received the database from MIS to begin the analyses, however, she discovered that personal name identifiers were automatically recorded for each respondent. Upon further inquiries, the psychologist learned from the MIS department that this was a necessary feature of E-mail intended to prevent fraudulent messages from being disseminated in another person's name. The MIS department's manager assured the psychologist that the identifiers would not be used to compromise any person's confidential responses. The psychologist decided to accept the word of the MIS department and to continue using the system, which, otherwise, appeared to be working well.

B. Ethics Code Standards

> **Ethical Standard 5.01   Discussing the Limits of Confidentiality**
>
> **(a) Psychologists discuss with persons and organizations with**

whom they establish a scientific or professional relationship
... (1) the relevant limitations on confidentiality ... in organizational consulting, and (2) the foreseeable uses of the
information generated through their services.
(b) Unless it is not feasible or is contraindicated, the discussion of confidentiality occurs at the onset of the relationship
and thereafter as new circumstances may warrant.

Ethical Standard 5.02   Maintaining Confidentiality

Psychologists have a primary obligation and take reasonable
precautions to respect the confidentiality rights of those with
whom they work or consult. . . .

Ethical Standard 5.04   Maintenance of Records

Psychologists maintain appropriate confidentiality in creating, storing, accessing, transferring, and disposing of records
under their control, whether these are written, automated, or
in any other medium. . . .

Ethical Standard 5.07   Confidential Information in Data-
bases

(a) If confidential information concerning recipients of psychological services is to be entered into databases or systems
of records available to persons whose access has not been
consented to by the recipient, then psychologists use coding
or other techniques to avoid the inclusion of personal identifiers.

C. Case Interpretation

In this case, it is not clear whether the psychologist had, in the planning
phases of the project, explicitly considered or asked the MIS department
whether any possible violation of confidentiality might occur. This would
have been a prudent starting point before using an untested methodology
to collect confidential information. The data might still have been obtained
in the manner described, but advance precautions could then have been
taken to protect the data as they were collected and perhaps to have the
data collection point be the psychologist rather than the MIS department.
At the least, respondents could have been informed that their name identifiers would be in place and of the precautions that would be taken to
assure anonymity of their data.

Once, well into the project, the existence of the identifying codes was
discovered, the psychologist could then have attempted to remedy the existing situation and to ensure that problems of this sort did not recur. In
handling the immediate project's data, the psychologist might immediately
have purged files of all respondent identifiers, assuring that this also hap-

pened with any copies of the data which were still in the possession of the MIS department. Should the MIS department not be responsive to this request, the psychologist might then have communicated the situation to management and attempted to work out an immediate remedy.

Concerning possible future survey administrations on the E-mail system, the psychologist would need to find a method to remove personal identifiers before the data were received or otherwise would need to inform the respondents about how and why the identifiers were collected and how the data were to be protected and stored. Other solutions, such as using shared centralized terminals rather than E-mail for data collection, may also be feasible.

D. Case Implications

Any new technology offers the promise of improved efficiency but inevitably has consequences, intended and otherwise. Psychologists wisely anticipate potential threats to promised conditions before embarking on the use of the technology. Trial runs of a new technique before the system is used on a broader scale are desirable.

Psychologists own the responsibility for assuring confidentiality when that has been promised or implied in the data collection effort. They should not rely on promises made by others, particularly those not bound by the same ethics code, regarding the protection of confidentiality. Psychologists generally need to anticipate the possible intended and unintended misuses of data, especially data collected in a previously untried format. The long-term protection of the data must also be taken into account, recognizing that the retention of data may extend beyond the tenure of the psychologist who is responsible for establishing and overseeing the system.

Case 18 _____

Maintaining Confidentiality in Survey Reporting

A. Statement of the Problem

An I/O psychologist was responsible for administering a corporate employee survey program. The employees were guaranteed anonymity. To help achieve this goal, the organization agreed not to report results of any group of employees that had less than five respondents.

Over the past several years, the organization has attempted to improve action planning and accountability for results by giving managers increased latitude for creating report specifications. The intention of this policy was to increase employees' understanding and use of survey results.

In reviewing one manager's requests for customized reports, the psychologist discovered that even though each report had five or more respondents, a comparison of the reports could potentially expose the responses of a particular employee whose input was in one report but not the other. The psychologist had no reason to believe that the report requests were made for the purpose of discovering employees' responses. In fact, it would require a fairly sophisticated user of survey results to be able to determine the responses of a particular person. The psychologist decided that the overall objectives of the survey program and the need to support management in the use of the results justified the delivery of the reports in the requested form. He therefore produced the reports as they had been ordered.

B. Ethics Code Standards

Ethical Standard 5.01   Discussing the Limits of Confidentiality

(a) Psychologists discuss with persons and organizations with whom they establish a scientific or professional relationship . . . (1) the relevant limitations on confidentiality, including limitations where applicable in . . . organizational consulting, and (2) the foreseeable uses of the information generated through their services.

Ethical Standard 5.02   Maintaining Confidentiality

Psychologists have a primary obligation and take reasonable precautions to respect the confidentiality rights of those with whom they work or consult, recognizing that confidentiality may be established by law, institutional rules, or professional or scientific relationships.

C. Case Interpretation

The psychologist in this case was bound by the promise of anonymity in the reporting of participants' survey input and results. At the same time, the psychologist had an obligation to the organization to comply with the policy of presenting survey results in such a way as to maximize the organization's investment in the process through the full use of available data.

Despite the fact that there was little likelihood that the individual's responses could be discovered through a comparison of two reports, the psychologist must anticipate this possibility and take action on that awareness. One solution would have been to inform the manager of the potential problem in general terms and to ask the manager to agree to use only one survey report. A second one would have been to decline to provide one of the reports and to provide the affected manager with an explanation that providing both reports would potentially have violated the anonymity promised to participants. Perhaps, as another alternative, results from more than one work group of the supervisor could have been combined with another one to have achieved the desired anonymity. The psychologist also should use the experience to work with the company's management to design the following year's survey in ways that might provide both specificity and protection to participants.

D. Case Implications

There are many instances in which psychologists must balance competing ethical interests and obligations. Ideally, courses of action can be identified that satisfy all parties. When this is not possible, the psychologist needs to consider alternative, satisficing rather than optimizing solutions.

When there are conflicts of the sort depicted in this case, the promise of anonymity for the individual generally needs to take precedence over the needs of the organization's managers for the requested data. While the managers had also been promised reports of their own design, the prior assurances of anonymity would take precedence if no compromise solution could be crafted.

Case 19

Implementing an Equitable Bonus Plan

A. Statement of the Problem

A company's compensation manager was asked by the vice president of HR to prepare a proposal for introducing a bonus plan for all exempt employees. The vice president asked the company's I/O psychologist to advise the company's compensation manager on the project.

Together the compensation manager and the psychologist developed a proposal for awarding annual bonuses to all executives if the company met both revenue and profit goals and to all other exempt employees if the company met its revenue goals. The proposal was presented to and accepted by the company's executive committee. The new plan was then widely publicized within the company.

Midway through the first year of the bonus plan, the company's vice president of finance reported that the company was likely to meet its revenue goals for the year but was unlikely to meet its profit goals due to the new bonus plan. Bonuses constituted a significant portion of the executives' income, yet in the last 2 years the bonuses had been scaled back due to increased operating costs and a business downturn. Executives were expecting restored bonuses this year. The vice president of finance therefore advised the HR vice president that the employee bonus plan would need to be severely scaled back and even dropped if necessary to preserve the executive bonuses.

The vice president of HR then met with the compensation manager and the psychologist to tell them about the new developments. He asked them to prepare a severely downscaled bonus plan and to alert employees of the distinct possibility that there might not be any bonuses for employees this year.

The psychologist strongly argued against such a course of action. The psychologist pointed out that the operating profit goal could not be reached without all the employees, not just the executives, and that reneging on a promise would clearly be a breach of promise with potentially serious implications. Moreover, the psychologist noted, employees would very likely deeply resent the action and possibly become much less cooperative in the future. The psychologist then offered to resign, citing the APA Ethics Code

Standard on "conflicts between ethics and organizational demands" and adding that it was critically important for everyone involved in the matter not to tarnish their integrity.

Probably inspired by the psychologist's stance, the compensation manager followed with essentially the same arguments and then suggested that the vice president for finance take the problem to the executive committee and make a plea for keeping the promise made to the employees. The vice president reluctantly agreed to do so and was surprised when the committee unanimously agreed to honor the commitment to the employees, even if that meant dramatically reducing bonuses for the executives. As it turned out, the company exceeded its goals by the end of the year, and all employees received full bonuses.

B. Ethics Code Standards

Ethical Standard 1.14   Avoiding Harm

Psychologists take reasonable steps to avoid harming their patients or clients, research participants, students, and others with whom they work, and to minimize harm where it is foreseeable and unavoidable.

Ethical Standard 8.03   Conflicts Between Ethics and Organizational Demands

If the demands of an organization with which psychologists are affiliated conflict with this Ethics Code, psychologists clarify the nature of the conflict, make known their commitment to the Ethics Code, and to the extent feasible, seek to resolve the conflict in a way that permits the fullest adherence to the Ethics Code.

C. Case Interpretation

The psychologist in this case was caught in a classical conflict between protesting and acquiescing to a proposition which was plausible to some in the organization but which the psychologist considered to be a breach of ethics. The psychologist took a forceful stand consistent with his views of the ethically appropriate thing to do in a complex situation. While not required by the Ethics Code, his offer to resign reinforced the importance he attached to the decision. In this instance, the behavior was rewarded when the matter came before the company's executive committee.

D. Case Implications

It is inevitable that psychologists will at different points in their careers face many temptations and pressures to behave in ways contrary to their ethical values. It can be particularly difficult to take a strong ethical stance when persons who take positions contrary to psychologists' ethical codes and values are in positions of great power and influence.

It is not necessary to take extreme positions, such as offering one's resignation, in every instance of ethical disagreement. Still, by persisting in articulating and, if necessary, fighting for an ethical viewpoint, psychologists enhance not only their own sense of well-being and professional self-esteem but also the well-being of others in the organization. They also teach that it is possible to achieve organizational goals while behaving ethically.

Case 20 _____

Conflicting Obligations in Survey Research

A. Statement of the Problem

An I/O psychologist conducted an employee opinion survey for one of his organizational clients, a large manufacturing corporation. As was the custom in this firm, the survey included a few places for written comments in addition to the many objective, forced-choice attitudinal items.

The company's policy was to guarantee anonymity to all respondents. Consistent with this policy, when written comments were entered into the computer, any names or other potential identifiers were deleted. All of the original written comments were then destroyed.

After the survey results were disseminated one of the managers noticed a written comment in the summary of the survey results stating that there was an unresolved safety issue in the organization that was potentially life threatening. The respondent insisted that management investigate the issue immediately and that the condition, over time, could be damaging. However, the respondent did not provide enough information to allow management to address the issue. The company asked the psychologist for assistance in obtaining the needed information.

Since all names and other identifiers had been destroyed, there was no possibility that survey information could be used to identify the respondent. The psychologist could attempt to identify the respondent using the demographic data in the survey (e.g., department, job, gender). However, he informed the company that he would not do so, since it would potentially violate the company's commitment to survey anonymity.

After considering the ethical issues he perceived to be associated with ignoring the safety issue versus those connected with violating the promise of anonymity, the psychologist decided that the safety issue still needed to be addressed. Rather than attempting to identify the respondent by name, he used the demographic data to identify a pool of 32 respondents that would include the respondent of interest. The psychologist sent every employee in this group a memo describing the situation, the company's commitment to preserving respondents' anonymity and to employee safety, and the need for more specific information regarding the safety issue. The memo asked any respondent with information about the reported safety problem anonymously or otherwise to forward the information to the company's director of safety.

B. Ethics Code Standards

Ethical Standard 5.02   Maintaining Confidentiality

Psychologists have a primary obligation . . . to respect the confidentiality rights of those with whom they work or consult. . . .

Ethical Standard 5.06   Consultations

When consulting with their colleagues, (1) psychologists do not share confidential information that reasonably could lead to the identification of a . . . client, research participant, or any other person or organization with whom they have a confidential relationship unless they have obtained the prior consent of the person or organization or the disclosure cannot be avoided.

C. Case Interpretation

The psychologist in this case faced a difficult ethical dilemma. He recognized the inherent conflict in ignoring the safety concern and violating the commitment to anonymity. Although it could be argued that the person making the claim of a safety violation had the obligation to bring it to management's attention in a manner other than an anonymous survey, the psychologist still felt an obligation not to ignore the alleged safety threat. In doing so, he was careful not to compromise, or to give survey respondents the impression of having compromised, respondent anonymity. The psychologist acted ethically in responding to the situation and in refusing simply to give management what was asked. He risked losing an organizational client by standing firm on upholding his ethical standards. Other ethical responses would also have been possible, including sending the letter to all survey respondents, not just the selected group of participants.

D. Case Implications

As this case highlights, psychologists may be placed in positions in which they have conflicting ethical obligations. There may be no unambiguously correct way to behave in such situations. When such situations arise, psychologists should carefully consider their various obligations and attempt to resolve the conflict in a way that will minimize harm to all parties involved. Innovative solutions may be needed to resolve the conflicts in an acceptable way.

Psychologists working with industrial clients often must work with company's managers who may be accustomed to their dictates being followed. Psychologists can maintain an ethical stance in such situations by assuming that adherence to ethical standards is a given, and considering requests made by persons in positions of authority in that context. Losing an organizational client may at times be a preferable outcome to behaving in ways that compromise the psychologist's principles.

Case 21

Protecting the Confidentiality of Upward Feedback

A. Statement of the Problem

A group of organizational psychologists who were working as internal consultants in a large energy company were asked to develop an upward feedback process for the company's managers. The purposes of this project were to establish a communication process by which subordinates anonymously could provide feedback to managers about perceived managerial behavior and style and to provide information the managers could use to improve their skills. Company officials also hoped to increase the managers' accountability for their behavior toward their subordinates by having quantitative information.

The psychologists collaborated on the project with the company's HR manager. The assumptions of the intervention were that the data collected were to be used *only* for the development of the managers, and as a basis for dialogue with their work groups. The plan was that managers develop personal action plans to respond to the identified issues. It was intended that no one would know an individual's feedback results other than the manager, the manager's boss, and the manager's work group, unless he or she chose to share them more broadly. It was also specifically stated that the managers were expected to share the data with their superiors.

After 2 years, the client company's HR manager requested that the psychologists conduct a study of leadership effectiveness based on the upward feedback process. He also wanted to showcase good leadership behavior by having the 20 managers with the highest scores on the feedback instrument identified and their names publicized. He wanted to improve the overall management style in the company by publicly recognizing those managers who were well regarded by their subordinates, interview them to better understand their approach to leadership practices, and then to publish these practices as a guide to other managers and leaders.

The psychologists actively resisted the HR manager's plan, and it was not put into effect. They suggested an alternative approach which would allow the study to be conducted without violating anyone's confidentiality.

B. Ethics Code Standards

Ethical Standard 5.01   Discussing the Limits of Confidentiality

(a) Psychologists discuss with persons and organizations with whom they establish scientific or professional relationship . . . (1) the relevant limitations on confidentiality . . . and (2) the foreseeable uses of the information generated through their services.

Ethical Standard 5.02   Maintaining Confidentiality

Psychologists have a primary obligation and take reasonable precautions to respect the confidentiality rights of those with whom they work or consult. . . .

Ethical Standard 5.06   Consultations

When consulting with their colleagues, (1) psychologists do not share confidential information that reasonably could lead to the identification of a . . . client, research participant, or any other person or organization with whom they have a confidential relationship unless they have obtained the prior consent of the person or organization or the disclosure cannot be avoided.

C. Case Interpretation

This case concerns the potential misuse of information obtained during the feedback process for purposes not originally agreed upon in the consulting project.

The HR manager's request presented a conflict. The intent of the project was to use upward feedback data for participants to learn more about their leadership behavior and thereby to improve their managerial effectiveness. Anonymity and confidentiality of data had been promised. Identifying the "top leaders" and publishing the results would violate the psychologists' promise of maintaining confidentiality of data. Not only would this information lead to identifying the top 20 managers with the highest feedback scores, but indirectly the approach would publicly expose those with lower scores without the prior agreement of any of the persons whose data were involved.

An additional issue concerns the effect such a disclosure would have on the upward feedback process in the future. Raters and participants might then consciously or unconsciously distort their rating if they knew that the results would be presented in a public forum.

The psychologists rightly acted to resist the plan. They suggested an alternative approach which would allow the study to be conducted without violating anyone's confidentiality.

D. Case Implications

Psychologists working with managers must constantly be alert to efforts to extend a program beyond its original reach. New ideas and revisions are an inevitable part of the managerial process. Often such efforts are made with the greatest of intentions and enthusiasm. Because persons voicing the suggested changes may be highly placed in the organization, they may have the power to implement their suggestions with little resistance.

It is the responsibility of psychologists to resist changes in an original agreement when those changes would result in behaviors that would be in violation of the ethics of the profession. Aggressive assertion may be needed to protect the original terms of the agreement.

Case 22 _____

Misuse of Psychological Services

A. Statement of the Problem

A Midwestern United States manufacturing company producing machine parts had been experiencing union–management conflict for many years. Union representatives had staged walkouts and strikes several times to voice their complaints over wages and working conditions, and although several concessions had been made by both parties in the area of wages and benefits, serious disagreements remained on issues of working conditions.

The company's senior management approached an I/O psychologist with the request that she assess the work situation and, on the basis of the obtained information, make a proposal for change. After an initial series of interviews, the I/O psychologist identified widespread concerns over safety and training. She recommended a more thorough needs assessment, which would be followed by specific safety training and job redesign efforts. The union response to the proposal was favorable, and management quickly agreed to sponsor the work. During ensuing contract negotiations, the union agreed to management's proposals with the understanding that the training and redesign efforts would be completed soon thereafter. It was agreed in the negotiations that the changes would be implemented with all due haste and would be fully in place within a year.

After about a month of starting to work on the plan's implementation, the I/O psychologist began to encounter delays and resistance from the management. Requests for necessary information were not fulfilled, and access to work situations was denied on several occasions. The rationale given was always suggestive of some plausible factor in the workplace that prevented the contact, though collectively the events suggested a systematic effort to prevent access. The coordinating members of the management team continued to assure the psychologist that the project would move ahead as planned but recommended that the proposal's original schedule be extended.

At the end of a meeting with some of the union shop stewards, one of the participants asked the psychologist what she knew about a rumor circulating that management intended to move the company to a country known for its cheap labor supply. After assuring the shop steward that she had heard nothing of such a plan, the I/O psychologist approached a senior manager to discuss the rumor.

The manager, quickly closing his office door, became visibly uneasy, asking the identity of the person who had made the statement, which the psychologist declined to reveal. The manager stated that he was not at liberty to discuss plans for the future of the company. He went on to tell the I/O psychologist that her project would continue through the next 6 months but that she should expect delays in the originally planned schedule.

The manager's remarks intimated that the psychologist had been brought in to appease the union and to forestall any further walkouts until management could finalize decisions about the future of the company. Before leaving the manager's office, the I/O psychologist was told that the information she had just received about the company's decisions about its future was to be kept in strictest confidence and that she was to deny the rumors of a move when talking with members of the union.

The psychologist informed the manager that she would not participate in the requested conspiracy of denial and that it would be professionally unethical for her to lie about something she felt sure to be true. After discussing the entire situation with several key managers in the firm, in which she voiced her several concerns about the project and management's intentions, and receiving no assurances that there would be real cooperation with her work, the I/O psychologist notified management that she was terminating her involvement with the company. She advised the union representatives of her departure and noted in general terms that she felt she could no longer be effective in working on the project. She did not comment further on her belief that management had no intentions of implementing the agreed-upon changes.

B. Ethics Code Standards

Ethical Standard 1.16   Misuse of Psychologists' Work

(a) Psychologists do not participate in activities in which it appears likely that their skills or data will be misused by others, unless corrective mechanisms are available. (See also Standard 7.04, Truthfulness and Candor.)
(b) If psychologists learn of misuse or misrepresentation of their work, they take reasonable steps to correct or minimize the misuse or misrepresentation.

Ethical Standard 3.03   Avoidance of False or Deceptive Statements

(a) Psychologists do not make public statements that are false, deceptive, misleading, or fraudulent, either because of what they state, convey, or suggest or because of what they omit, concerning their research, practice, or other work activities or those of persons or organizations with which they are affiliated. . . .

Ethical Standard 4.09 Terminating the Professional Relationship

(b) Psychologists terminate a professional relationship when it becomes reasonably clear that the . . . client no longer needs the service, is not benefiting, or is being harmed by continued service.

Ethical Standard 8.03 Conflicts Between Ethics and Organizational Demands

If the demands of an organization with which psychologists are affiliated conflict with this Ethics Code, psychologists clarify the nature of the conflict, make known their commitment to the Ethics Code, and to the extent feasible, seek to resolve the conflict in a way that permits the fullest adherence to the Ethics Code.

C. Case Interpretation

The case involves a conflict between the two different consumers of psychological services. As the contracting agent and payer for the services, the company's management was the primary client in this case. However, the union was an important consumer of the services as well. Its members were an important part of the data collection effort and were directly affected by the training and job redesign services agreed to be provided.

The agreement entered into by all three of these parties was based on the understanding that the psychological services would be implemented for the primary intended benefit of the union employees. In fact, management was apparently attempting to use the agreement to give the appearance of addressing the union's concerns while contemplating whether to relocate the firm. In addition, the I/O psychologist was indirectly being asked by the manager of the company to mislead the union members by withholding information and denying knowledge of the company's plans.

Any attempt to use the I/O psychologist's services in a way that was deceptive or misleading would compromise the ethical standards of the I/O psychologist and the reputation of both the psychologist and the profession. In this case, the I/O psychologist made a decision to resolve the conflict between the organization's demands and the ethical standards of the psychological profession by leaving the situation. Before making this decision, however, she made several attempts to address the issues directly.

Since the union was also a party to the project, the psychologist was placed in a difficult dilemma in her decision to terminate her involvement with the project. Her belief that management was not serious about doing the work was reasonable under the circumstances. However, the manager's attempt to bind her to silence about even the general information she had received placed her in a difficult situation. Without violating requested confidentiality, she could not fully explain her reasons for leaving the company.

In this case, the decision to leave the company may not have required a detailed explanation to communicate to union and management alike its intended message. On the other hand, the issue might have been anticipated as a possible outcome of a highly conflictual initial situation, and arrangements at the outset of the project for terminating the relationship if there were not mutual cooperation could have been made.

D. Case Implications

I/O psychologists have a responsibility to clarify with contracting parties the nature of a consulting relationship. Anticipating the areas of potential ethical conflict at the beginning of a project helps to minimize the possibility of later undesirable outcomes. In situations known to be conflictual, there is a particular obligation to consider possible situations that might arise and make appropriate contingency plans.

One clear area that should be of concern to psychologists in any applied project is how the results of a psychological or organizational intervention will be used. This is particularly true when there is known controversy or a history of adverse action. No matter what the intended end results of an intervention, there is still the obligation to assess carefully the potential for damage to relevant groups and persons in the organization before agreeing to undertake an assignment.

Despite the best of intentions, and the best of plans, unanticipated situations do arise in the course of consulting work that may create ethical dilemmas. Then, the psychologist must address the changed circumstances, difficult, conflictual, and unpleasant though they may be. Termination of a consulting engagement is not to be undertaken for trivial reasons, but when all reasonable efforts to resolve what has become a difficult situation fail, it may be the psychologist's responsibility to end the project rather than to risk an even greater harm.

Case 23 _____

Confidentiality of Interview Data

A. Statement of the Problem

A psychologist was retained by a company to help reduce conflict between management and labor. As a first step, the psychologist conducted a series of interviews with nonmanagement employees. It was agreed by the organizational representatives and the psychologist that the content and results of all individual interviews would be kept confidential and that the psychologist would make only general programmatic recommendations based on the overall findings.

During the course of these interviews, it became apparent that one supervisor in particular was the perceived cause of considerable conflict. Shortly after finishing the interviews, the psychologist learned that one of the interviewees had been fired by the supervisor. The terminated employee had asserted during the interview that the supervisor had been engaging in systematic verbal and emotional harassment. This assertion was corroborated by other interviewees.

In addition to registering harassment charges with a relevant government agency, the fired employee filed a grievance with the union. The complaint went through several steps in a written format and finally reached the stage of binding arbitration. A hearing was scheduled, and an outside arbitrator was contracted to hear the case. Each side was allowed to present its case, and witnesses could be called to provide corroborating or disconfirming evidence.

The grievant contacted the psychologist to come to the arbitration session to support his claims of harassment and unfair and retaliatory termination. The psychologist declined to testify, noting that it would violate his confidentiality obligations to the persons interviewed. The complainant stated that he felt the psychologist was taking management's side in the matter.

B. Ethics Code Standards

Ethical Standard 1.14   Avoiding Harm

Psychologists take reasonable steps to avoid harming their . . . clients . . . and others with whom they work, and to minimize harm where it is foreseeable and unavoidable.

Ethical Standard 5.01   Discussing the Limits of Confidentiality

(a) Psychologists discuss with persons and organizations with whom they establish a scientific, or professional relationship . . . (1) the relevant limitations on confidentiality, including limitations where applicable in . . . organizational consulting, and (2) the foreseeable uses of the information generated through their services.

(b) Unless it is not feasible or is contraindicated, the discussion of confidentiality occurs at the outset of the relationship and thereafter as new circumstances may warrant.

Ethical Standard 5.02   Maintaining Confidentiality

Psychologists have a primary obligation and take reasonable precautions to respect the confidentiality rights of those with whom they work or consult, recognizing that confidentiality may be established by law, institutional rules, or professional or scientific relationships.

Ethical Standard 5.05   Disclosures

(a) Psychologists disclose confidential information without the consent of the individual only as mandated by law, or where permitted by law for a valid purpose, such as . . . to protect the patient or client or others from harm. . . .

(b) Psychologists also may disclose confidential information with the appropriate consent of the . . . individual or organizational client (or of another legally authorized person on behalf of the . . . client), unless prohibited by law.

C. Case Interpretation

The psychologist in this case had an obligation to respect the confidentiality of the information obtained during the course of the interviews, and this obligation extended both to the interviewees and to individuals named during the interviews. The psychologist was also obligated to protect the rights of the client contracting for psychological services. In this case, the company was the primary client, but the interviewees and those persons named during the interviews were also affected parties. Certainly the psychologist might reasonably have approached the client organization's representatives, presented the circumstances, and allowed the opportunity to respond to the individual's request.

Although the agreement that the interview data would be kept confidential was primarily designed to protect the interviewees, in this instance, confidentiality actually worked to the perceived disadvantage of one of them, the terminated employee. Still, the prior agreement had specified that the content of the interviews would remain confidential. Additionally, were the psychologist to share the information from the interviews, those individuals might have been retaliated against as well (assuming the claims made by the terminated employee were accurate). The welfare of the supervisor was also involved, since a successful charge of harassment that was supported by the psychologist's data might have meant his dismissal. Finally, the primary client in this case, the company, still had its original problem to be solved.

The psychologist, by choosing to maintain the confidentiality of the interviews, made a difficult choice between the principle of confidentiality and the perceived interests of the interviewee. For the psychologist to use the interview data to support the employee's charges of harassment would likely undermine the credibility of both the psychologist and the company executives who represented the primary client. In making this decision, the psychologist also took into account the fact that the same information obtained during the interviews might otherwise be obtained in the hearing and that at best the psychologist would be reporting hearsay information. Were the psychologist subpoenaed to testify at a legal proceeding, testimony might then be compelled.

Of course there were other opportunities open to the psychologist concerning the information he obtained about the offending supervisor. In summarizing the information obtained from the interviews, which, after all, focused on labor–management relations, the psychologist had an opportunity to present the findings in a way that might help the organization address its problem managers in a more systematic way. This was the primary purpose for the project in the first place and where the psychologist's efforts stood the greatest likelihood of having impact. Also, without addressing specifics of the situation, the psychologist might be able to help management understand that the incident itself reflected management–labor problems needing to be addressed on a more systematic basis.

D. Case Implications

It is always desirable to anticipate the things that can go wrong in a consulting relationship and to take appropriate preventative actions. Of course, it is never possible to anticipate every contingency or potential problem, but the general principles governing the relationship need to be clearly communicated in the planning stages.

Before undertaking a project in which sensitive data are likely to be collected (and almost every conflictual labor–management interaction should be assumed to have that possibility), the psychologist should establish clear ground rules as to how the data will be maintained and how results will be communicated to all parties. When individually collected information is promised to be kept confidential, it becomes the psychologist's obligation to keep that promise. When it can reasonably be anticipated that data collected under terms of confidentiality might become part of a legal proceeding, the psychologist should make such possibilities known to participants at the outset of their participation.

Case 24

Team-Building Interventions

A. Statement of the Problem

A participant in a team-building exercise was singled out by the I/O psychologist-facilitator as a "troublesome" member. The psychologist, who had trained in traditional areas of personnel psychology and who began doing the team building a few years prior to this exercise but with little formal training in the area, asked the participant to remove himself physically from the group. He was asked to turn his chair away from the group while the psychologist led a discussion of the negative aspects of the participant's behavior in the exercise. Upon returning to the group, the participant became an inactive team member throughout the balance of the exercise. The individual left the group angry, hurt, and with little meaningful learning having occurred. Some time after the experience, the participant bitterly and emotionally recollected the treatment, suggesting that long-term negative attitudes resulted from the experience.

B. Ethics Code Standards

Ethical Standard 1.04   Boundaries of Competence

(a) Psychologists provide services, teach, and conduct research only within the boundaries of their competence, based on their education, training, supervised experience, or appropriate professional experience.
(b) Psychologists provide services . . . or conduct research in new areas or involving new techniques only after first undertaking appropriate study, training, supervision, and/or consultation from persons who are competent in those areas or techniques.

Ethical Standard 1.14   Avoiding Harm

Psychologists take reasonable steps to avoid harming their . . . clients . . . and others with whom they work, and to minimize harm where it is foreseeable and unavoidable.

C. Case Interpretation

The facilitator, as a professional psychologist, had the responsibility to protect the dignity and well-being of the participants in the team development intervention. Many team development programs such as the one in this case appropriately rely on the behavior of the members of the team as the basis for the participant becoming aware of the impact of his or her behavior on others. When constructively analyzed by staff leaders and other team members in a supportive and constructive environment, participants' behavior becomes the framework for attempting to improve interpersonal and managerial styles. Because such learning can be emotionally demanding, it is important that the facilitator be well trained in such work. The psychologist must assume responsibility for maintaining an environment that is supportive rather than destructive and that appropriately handles situations which could otherwise be humiliating to participants or serve to lower their self-esteem.

The facilitator's responsibility for minimizing the likelihood of psychological casualties by the participants is especially important. In this case, the facilitator, an I/O psychologist, appeared to have ignored his ethical responsibility to protect a participant's psychological well-being. The participant might have learned a great deal from the effects the "troublesome" behavior was having on others; instead, the facilitator actively encouraged the team to isolate the individual. If negative feedback were essential to the participant's learning, or to the well-being of the group, the psychologist should have helped the member understand it and deal with the member's emotional reactions to the criticism. The psychologist should also help the other team members understand the role they may be playing in precipitating the behavior.

There is also a question raised in this case about the psychologist's fitness for doing this type of work at all. It would appear that he was not adequately trained for this assignment and should have had considerably more supervised training, particularly on the affective issues, before offering such services to persons in organizations or other settings. This was a new area of work for this psychologist, and appropriate training and supervision should have been sought before undertaking this activity.

D. Case Implications

Organizational development interventions such as team building present special challenges since psychologists of several areas of specialization may, with appropriate training and experience, provide such services. Regardless of the psychologist's primary area of specialization, however, the facilitator must conduct such experiences ethically and competently, setting an appropriate role model.

Failure to attend to the needs of specific team members who are persistently being scapegoated or isolated from the team demonstrates limited understanding by the facilitator of the potential power groups can have even on psychologically healthy individuals. Psychologists learning such techniques as team building, group facilitation, and conflict resolution should be fully trained, including supervised experience, to minimize the likelihood of their engendering psychological problems on the part of team participants.

As the boundaries between areas of specialty blur, it becomes more difficult to determine fitness for particular kinds of work. Just as I/O psychologists rightly complain about clinical and counseling psychologists practicing industrial applications without benefit of training, so clinicians have cause for alarm when I/O psychologists move into clinical domains without appropriate preparation. "Executive coaching" provides an example of a wide-ranging set of activities with much potential for I/O psychologists to cross their boundaries of competence into clinical and counseling areas. It is not the case that such work should never be able to be done by I/O psychologists. Combining specialties into new hybrids can serve many useful purposes. However, ethical issues are raised when psychologists begin practice in areas they wish to add to their skill base without benefit of formal training or other preparation.

Case 25 _____

Misuse of Employee Opinion Surveys to Prevent Unionization

A. Statement of the Problem

A nonunion manufacturing firm, located in a heavily unionized state, was concerned about the possibility of employee organization and eventual unionization of the firm. In an attempt to retain its nonunion status, management hired an I/O psychologist, who was assigned the responsibility of administering employee opinion surveys. The surveys were administered to employees with the assurance that their individual answers would be kept confidential and that all summaries of data would be grouped so that individual respondents could never be identified.

In fact, the surveys were constructed in such a way as to allow identification of possible union activists among the existing workforce as well as among job applicants. The psychologist then reported to management the names of alleged activists. Subtle pressure was then applied by management resulting in the eventual termination of current employees, or, in the case of job applicants, the refusal to hire. Eventually, the underlying purpose of the employee opinion surveys was detected by the employees, and the I/O psychologist terminated employment with the firm.

B. Ethics Code Standards

Ethical Standard 1.09   Respecting Others

In their work-related activities, psychologists respect the rights of others to hold values, attitudes, and opinions that differ from their own.

Ethical Standard 1.15   Misuse of Psychologists' Influence

Because psychologists' scientific and professional judgments and actions may affect the lives of others, they are alert to and guard against personal, financial, social, organizational, or political factors that might lead to misuse of their influence.

Ethical Standard 1.16   Misuse of Psychologists' Work

(a) Psychologists do not participate in activities in which it appears likely that their skills or data will be misused by others, unless corrective mechanisms are available.

(b) If psychologists learn of misuse or misrepresentation of their work, they take reasonable steps to correct or minimize the misuse or misrepresentation.

Ethical Standard 2.02   Competence and Appropriate Use of Assessments and Interventions

(b) Psychologists refrain from misuse of assessment techniques, interventions, results, and interpretations and take reasonable steps to prevent others from misusing the information these techniques provide. . . .

Ethical Standard 5.02   Maintaining Confidentiality

Psychologists have a primary obligation and take reasonable precautions to respect the confidentiality rights of those with whom they work or consult, recognizing that confidentiality may be established by law, institutional rules, or professional or scientific relationships.

Ethical Standard 6.07   Responsibility

(a) Psychologists conduct research competently and with due concern for the dignity and welfare of the participants.

C. Case Interpretation

This case presents a clear violation of the obligation to protect confidentiality. The psychologist also egregiously colluded with management in the misuse of psychological techniques, potentially jeopardizing the reputation of the profession.

Apparently from the beginning of his affiliation with the firm and in the course of his professional activities, the psychologist knew that he was being asked to perform professionally inappropriate activities. He failed to inform management of the possible legal and ethical outcomes of the practice of secretly using survey data ostensibly collected for another purpose. It is assumed that the psychologist was fully cognizant of the fact that the professional psychological knowledge, skills, and services were potentially contributing to discriminatory and exploitative, if not illegal, practices. (If the psychologist was not, this in itself suggests a possible ethical violation.) The psychologist had the ethical obligation not to assume this role or to resign the position if he could not convince management to change its behavior.

The psychologist also blatantly ignored the responsibility to protect the confidentiality of information obtained from individual employees and applicants. Survey participants reasonably would assume, and in this case were explicitly advised, that their results would be kept confidential. By violating this sacred trust (and in some states, legal obligation), the psychologist seriously abused the participants' rights.

In his behavior, the psychologist also ignored the professional responsibility to maintain high professional standards. By his actions, he undermined the participants' trust for survey measurement, and potentially for the field of psychology as a whole.

D. Case Implications

There is no question that unethical behavior such as that manifested in this case has potentially far-reaching consequences beyond the individual employees and applicants who may be adversely affected by the behavior described. Psychologists consulting to organizations need to take an active role in challenging practices inconsistent with psychologists' ethical standards. If they are unsuccessful in changing behavior that is illegal or discriminatory, they have the right, and in many cases the ethical obligation, to terminate their affiliations.

Case 26 _____

Sharing of Management Development Results

A. *Statement of the Problem*

A psychologist employed by a large company designed and implemented a program for the development of managers. In the early stages of the project, a number of measures derived from commonly used executive development exercises were used to identify managers with strong and weak skills in particular aspects of management such as negotiations and task prioritizing. As the program progressed, the measures and exercises were revised and refined on each group of new management development participants. Normative data were collected throughout the program, and eventually the final measures were standardized and validated using a content validity strategy. Throughout the program, participants were told that the information obtained in the management development program was for developmental purposes only and would not be reviewed by their management.

After the program had been in use for some time, the psychologist who developed the management development program received a call from an executive who indirectly supervised several employees who had participated in the developmental assessment program. The executive asked to review the assessment results of all participants from his segment of the organization, so that he could ensure appropriate developmental experiences were planned on the job. The executive further explained that he also intended to use the results of the program to evaluate how effectively immediate supervisors, who had not seen the assessment results, had determined their subordinates' developmental needs. Because the results were to be used for developmental purposes, and would not be part of a formal evaluation process, the psychologist provided the executive with summary information regarding each individual's performance. He allowed the executive to review the information only in his office. He explained the limitations of the data, insisted that the information be kept confidential, and obtained a written consent that the information provided would not be used for purposes of evaluation.

B. Ethics Code Standards

Ethical Standard 2.02   Competence and Appropriate Use of Assessments and Interventions

(b) Psychologists refrain from misuse of assessment techniques, interventions, results, and interpretations and take reasonable steps to prevent others from misusing the information these techniques provide. This includes refraining from releasing raw test results or raw data to persons, other than to . . . clients as appropriate, who are not qualified to use such information. . . .

Ethical Standard 2.03   Test Construction

Psychologists who develop and conduct research with tests and other assessment techniques use scientific procedures and current professional knowledge for test design, standardization, validation, reduction or elimination of bias, and recommendations for use.

Ethical Standard 5.01   Discussing the Limits of Confidentiality

(a) Psychologists discuss with persons and organizations with whom they establish a . . . professional relationship . . . (1) the relevant limitations on confidentiality, including limitations where applicable in . . . organizational consulting, and (2) the foreseeable uses of the information generated through their services.
(b) Unless it is not feasible or is contraindicated, the discussion of confidentiality occurs at the outset of the relationship and thereafter as new circumstances may warrant.

Ethical Standard 5.02   Maintaining Confidentiality

Psychologists have a primary obligation and take reasonable precautions to respect the confidentiality rights of those with whom they work or consult, recognizing that confidentiality may be established by law, institutional rules, or professional or scientific relationships.

C. Case Interpretation

In this case, a psychologist gave an executive information that had been collected for developmental purposes. Since, among other reasons, the participants from whom the data were obtained were promised confidentiality, the psychologist acted inappropriately by releasing the information in any form to the executive. The psychologist should have recognized that no matter what promises obtained, he would lose control over the use of the data once they were released and should also have made the executive aware of the ethical issues involved in considering whether to provide the requested assessment information. Additionally, whatever possibilities there may have been to share the information with others in the company would have had to have been communicated at the outset of the project.

A second ethical issue in this case concerns the validation of the instruments. The psychologist had an ethical obligation to use only those psychological instruments that had been validated for the intended purposes. Although the psychologist eventually made efforts to validate all the instruments in the final assessment battery, he used measures that in the early stages of the project had not been validated at all. In addition, the psychologist had an obligation to keep accurate records for normative information and to assure that the normative data ware appropriately collected. In general, data collected from exercises that have been substantially altered from one administration to the next should not be retained in the normative base.

A third ethical issue involves an aspect of validation. The executive stated that he intended to use the data to evaluate how well the immediate supervisors diagnosed their subordinates' strengths and weaknesses. The psychologist should have warned the executive against this misuse of the management development data. There was no evidence that the assessment tools were an accurate measure of supervisors' personal appraisals of their subordinates. Since assessment exercises often place participants in roles that are not part of the individual's present job and require demonstrating behavior that may not easily be observed in day-to-day activities by the immediate supervisor, there is little assurance that they will be useful in evaluating supervisors' appraisal of their subordinates. On the basis of this characteristic alone, the psychologist should have resisted releasing the data since it is highly likely that under such circumstances they would be misused.

Finally, the psychologist might have explored in detail the executive's *current* need for evaluation of his employees. This focus could potentially have helped to direct attention from the information already collected under certain promised conditions to the manager's current needs for which psychological expertise might have been relevant. Careful exploration of these issues might have decreased any potential for power struggles over the release of the already-collected data.

D. Case Implications

Before collecting any assessment information on employees or other participants, psychologists should consider in some detail the likely uses to which such data might be put. The intended and potential uses of the data should be clarified with all concerned parties including participants, their supervisors and other executives, and personnel officials, and they should be offered the opportunity to participate or not based on that information.

It is the psychologist's responsibility to take an active role in establishing policy for the use of such data. He or she should outline any areas of ethical conflict with respect to the conditions under which data are collected and how the data will be used. The psychologist should validate assessment tools for the purposes for which the tools are intended to be used. Measures used for purposes of "development" are not exempt from requirements of validity simply because they are not used for purposes of selection.

Psychologists should expect that it is likely that those in positions of authority or others may, sometimes with the best of intentions, attempt to obtain and use data for other than their originally intended purposes. When such requests suggest a potential misuse of the data or results, it is the psychologist's responsibility actively to resist the request.

Case 27

Disposition of Psychological Reports

A. Statement of the Problem

Upon completion of a comprehensive organizational diagnostic study, an I/O psychologist prepared a report containing confidential and sensitive information including psychological profiles of key executives. The report was prepared in duplicate, with one copy given to the CEO of the client corporation for the executive's personal information and use and the second copy retained by the psychologist. Although the report was marked "confidential," the psychologist did not discuss the storage or disposition of the report with the executive receiving it, nor were there any specific instructions about its limitations or storage requirements noted in the report itself.

Several years later, after the company had been acquired by another firm, the psychologist was approached by the acquiring firm's CEO, with whom the psychologist was consulting on another matter. The CEO complimented the psychologist on his earlier report. In the course of the conversation, the psychologist discovered that the former CEO, upon leaving the firm, had left the report for his successor. The new CEO subsequently read the report and shared information from the report with other staff members. Believing that the report identified some important issues in managing some particular key employees, the executive circulated a copy of the report to several of his colleagues and had copies of sections from the report put in the relevant personnel files.

B. Ethics Code Standards

Ethical Standard 5.01   Discussing the Limits of Confidentiality

(a) Psychologists discuss with persons and organizations with whom they establish a scientific or professional relationship . . . (1) the relevant limitations on confidentiality, including limitations where applicable in . . . organizational consulting, and (2) the foreseeable uses of the information generated through their services.
(b) Unless it is not feasible or is contraindicated, the discus-

sion of confidentiality occurs at the outset of the relationship and thereafter as new circumstances may warrant.

Ethical Standard 5.02   Maintaining Confidentiality

Psychologists have a primary obligation and take reasonable precautions to respect the confidentiality rights of those with whom they work or consult, recognizing that confidentiality may be established by law, institutional rules, or professional or scientific relationships.

Ethical Standard 5.04   Maintenance of Records

Psychologists maintain appropriate confidentiality in creating, storing, accessing, transferring, and disposing of records under their control, whether these are written, automated, or in any other medium. Psychologists maintain and dispose of records in accordance with law and in a manner that permits compliance with the requirements of this Ethics Code.

C. Case Interpretation

This case provides a good example of the problems faced by psychologists in maintaining confidentiality in their work as consultants to organizations. The I/O psychologist in this case did provide the results of the study to an appropriate person and did maintain confidentiality of his own file copy of the report. However, the psychologist neglected to formalize with the former CEO the manner in which such information should be stored or disposed of.

Because psychologists in consulting roles are likely to be in their positions on a more or less temporary basis, the psychologist in this case should have tried to anticipate some of the possible outcomes to confidential or sensitive information after his departure from the firm or his engagement with other projects there. The psychologist should have been attentive to the possible misuse of reports by subsequent company officials and written the report in a way that would bring no avoidable harm to the subjects of the report. When obtaining confidential information, the psychologist should have made it clear to the executives that a report about them would be prepared for the CEO.

Even if he had been more explicit about requirements for the disposition of the report, the psychologist should have recognized that once a report had been released to a company, it was essentially outside of the psychologist's control. The psychologist should have written the report with this in mind. Such reports need to be technically accurate at the time of their preparation, but also reviewed by the psychologist from the perspective of possible misinterpretation. The possibility of how such reports would hold up to legal scrutiny should also be considered.

D. Case Implications

When releasing confidential information, particularly sensitive information that has the potential to be misused, it is in the best interests of all concerned to clarify what will happen to the information after it has been reviewed by the contracting company's representatives. This involves clarifying in very specific terms who has access to the psychological information, including whether persons being assessed are allowed to review the report, and what will happen to any written materials after the termination of the project. These terms should be expressed both in oral and written communication. A statement as to the sensitive nature of the material could also be included on the cover and individual pages of such a report, accompanied, on the cover, by specific provisions for storage or disposal of the information.

The psychologist and persons being assessed are somewhat protected from future problems by the preparation of accurate reports which clearly separate speculation from factual findings and which specify the circumstances under which the report was prepared. Nevertheless, there are multiple opportunities for misusing psychological data (particularly concerning individual employees) in organizational contexts by laypersons, so expectations of protection of confidentiality of a psychological report cannot be assumed.

Even when psychological consultants function with the organization as the intended client, they must still respect the rights of the individuals who may subsequently be damaged by the information included in a psychological report. Moreover, if psychologists gather information from many parts of an organization but their reports will be provided only to a CEO, the participants might well be informed of this prior to their involvement with the psychologist. Finally, psychologists preparing confidential reports for organizations need to anticipate that the persons with whom they work will not be in the organization forever and any assumptions about the role of such individuals in protecting sensitive psychological data from misuse are valid only as long as those individuals' tenure in the organization. Explicit provisions for the disposition of their reports are therefore critical in all organizational work.

Part III

Managing Consulting Relationships

Case 28 —————————————————

Avoiding Conflicts of Interests and Roles

A. Statement of the Problem

An I/O psychologist employed by a complex multinational corporation was responsible for developing and implementing executive development programs for the company. He created one such program with the assistance of an outside consultant, also a psychologist, who had a national reputation for such work. The consultant was also a faculty member at a local university where he was responsible for recruiting adjunct and part-time faculty.

After the contract work had been completed, the consultant, acting without additional input from his university colleagues, or from his employer, offered, and the corporate psychologist accepted, a teaching assignment at a rate of remuneration that was twice what competing universities offered for instruction of similar courses and much higher than what the university itself paid for similar adjunct teaching assignments. Other part-time faculty members were unaware of the pay differential.

B. Ethics Code Standards

Ethical Standard 1.15   Misuse of Psychologists' Influence

Because psychologists' scientific and professional judgments and actions may affect the lives of others, they are alert to and guard against personal, financial, social, organizational, or political factors that might lead to misuse of their influence.

Ethical Standard 1.16   Misuse of Psychologists' Work

(a) Psychologists do not participate in activities in which it appears likely that their skills or data will be misused by others, unless corrective mechanisms are available.
(b) If psychologists learn of misuse or misrepresentation of

their work, they take reasonable steps to correct or minimize the misuse or misrepresentation.

Ethical Standard 1.17   Multiple Relationships

(a) In many communities and situations, it may not be feasible or reasonable for psychologists to avoid social or other nonprofessional contacts with persons such as . . . clients . . . [or] supervisees. . . . Psychologists must always be sensitive to the potential harmful effects of other contacts on their work and on those persons with whom they deal. A psychologist refrains from entering into or promising another personal, scientific, professional, financial, or other relationship with such persons if it appears likely that such a relationship reasonably might impair the psychologist's objectivity or otherwise interfere with the psychologist's effectively performing his or her function as a psychologist. . . .
(b) Likewise, whenever feasible, a psychologist refrains from taking on professional or scientific obligations when preexisting relationships would create a risk of such harm.

C. Case Interpretation

One issue raised in this case is whether or not there was a conflict of interest associated with the consulting psychologist's multiple responsibilities. At least a potential conflict arises if, either during or soon after the teaching assignment, the consulting psychologist continued to provide services under contract to the corporate psychologist. The situation was especially problematic if the consultant not only recruited but also evaluated and decided whether to renew the contracts of adjunct faculty. In evaluating faculty performance, it was unlikely that objectivity could have been assured either by the university-affiliated consultant or by the corporate psychologist because of the complex and multiple relationships. The corporate psychologist might in such circumstances have been unduly influenced to favor the consultant for future contracts because of the preferential treatment he received in the teaching role. Conversely, differential treatment may have been given the corporate psychologist when functioning in the teaching role.

A second issue in this case concerns whether or not it was ethically appropriate for the consultant to have offered the teaching post to the corporate psychologist. Regardless of the specific motivations, there remained at least the appearance of atypically favorable terms having been associated with the teaching assignment. This action raises the possibility that the motivation may be more closely tied to the hope of future contracts rather than to the teaching need.

In evaluating the behavior described in this case, factors to be considered include the nature of the ongoing relationship, the credentials of both professionals relative to the specific work they were being asked to do, and the availability of other qualified psychologists to perform the teaching, consulting, and evaluation roles. At the least, the psychologist hiring adjunct faculty should, prior to binding the university to a financial commitment, have sought consultation from university colleagues on the decision to hire and on the remuneration issues. Alternatively, recognizing the multiple relationships involved, the psychologist might have been best advised to have another university administrator or faculty member negotiate the entire transaction and to evaluate the teaching performance. Similarly, if the consulting psychologist is considered for any additional projects the corporate psychologist could have another individual in the organization evaluate the consultant and negotiate the contract.

Finally, the corporate psychologist, in a complex issue and set of relationships, did not consult his employer. The new assignment could have affected his professional obligations to the company. For example, having to teach at a set time each week might have interfered with his travel schedule. The special treatment he was being given could also have affected relationships between the company and the university; the psychologist's supervisor should have been engaged in the decision-making process.

D. Case Implications

While it is not unethical per se to act in a way that is consistent with one's own perceived self-interests, care must be taken to assure that conflicts of interest, or potential conflicts of interest, do not impair judgment. When, as in this case, there exists a clear potential for conflicts of interest, psychologists are advised to carefully consider whether multiple relationships are prohibited, and to seek outside consultation to be sure that perceptual distortions have not influenced the decisions being made. If the circumstances permit, making public the negotiated terms, or at least the process used to establish those terms, may also help to minimize potential problems. Special care must be taken to manage not just the process used to reach an agreement but also the perceptions of others that based on a special relationship, preferential treatment may have influenced the outcome.

Case 29 _____

Accurately Reporting
Research Results

A. *Statement of the Problem*

An I/O psychologist in consulting practice was contracted by a company to study predictors of absenteeism. As a recent graduate, the psychologist was attempting to build up her practice and frankly needed the work. In a subtle way, the psychologist exaggerated what the client might expect as a result of the study she proposed to do, implying that the company might experience a significant decrease in absenteeism by agreeing to fund the study and implement its recommendations.

As her proposal stipulated, the psychologist reviewed the literature, identified a large number of potentially relevant variables, and prepared a study which required employees to complete a lengthy questionnaire. After the data were collected, the psychologist conducted complex multi-variate analyses which yielded only a small correlation with absenteeism.

The psychologist felt that if all the results were reported, the inability to say anything conclusive would have been professionally embarrassing, particularly after the expectations she had helped to create in marketing her project. Her report was therefore not very detailed concerning the technical analyses that were performed. She reported none of the empirical correlations of the survey variables with absenteeism. Instead, the psychologist organized the report around meta-analyses of the absenteeism literature. To make the report seem more customized, she added a number of anecdotes from interviews with selected employees.

The managers who had contracted for the study were not very pleased with the psychologist's report. They felt that they had not received what they had been promised in her proposal and that the report provided little locally relevant information they could not have obtained in-house at considerably less expense.

A key manager in the company confronted the psychologist with his concerns. At this point, the psychologist acknowledged that the results of the empirical analyses had been inconclusive and that she had therefore left most of them out. She also stated that she wanted the report to be understandable by the company officials and had therefore excluded some of the technical jargon.

The manager insisted that the report be rewritten to report all the work that had been in the original contract. The company's representatives remained unhappy with the revised final report she submitted. They still found little of use to the company, though at least the actual work performed by the psychologist was now summarized.

In response to the dissatisfaction, the coordinating manager in the company stated that the firm would not pay for the psychologist's originally contracted rate. Unhappily and after considerable protest of unfairness and unprofessionalism, the psychologist reluctantly agreed to the reduced payment. She feared that if she did not accept the revised terms, her professional reputation would suffer, and she wanted to end the dispute as painlessly and quietly as possible.

B. Ethics Code Standards

Ethical Standard 1.07   Describing the Nature and Results of Psychological Services

(a) When psychologists provide . . . consultation, research, or other psychological services to . . . an organization, they provide, using language that is reasonably understandable to the recipient of those services, appropriate information beforehand about the nature of such services and appropriate information later about results and conclusions.

Ethical Standard 1.23   Documentation of Professional and Scientific Work

(a) Psychologists appropriately document their professional and scientific work in order to facilitate provision of services later by them or by other professionals, to ensure accountability, and to meet other requirements of institutions or the law.

Ethical Standard 6.07   Responsibility

(a) Psychologists conduct research competently. . . .

Ethical Standard 6.21   Reporting of Results

(a) Psychologists do not fabricate data or falsify results in their publications.

C. Case Interpretation

The psychologist suppressed nonconfirming research findings. She attempted to mask the fact that her study yielded little information that had practical relevance for her organizational client. She erred not in relying on a meta-analytic procedure to make her recommendations, but in not delivering what she had promised and then attempting to disguise her actual findings.

A large part of the ethical problems in this case can be attributed to the manner in which the psychologist obtained the work with the company. She misled her potential client by implying that positive results could be assured from her work and by not educating the managers to the scientific reality that negative results were a possible outcome.

It would have been ethically desirable to have proposed the meta-analytic strategy in the first place, particularly if the available sample sizes in the company were small. This might have resulted in more statistically powerful conclusions than the ones possible with her data set. Or a combination of meta-analytic and empirical strategies might have been proposed.

The psychologist might still have rescued the situation when the negative results became apparent if she had then advised her client of the results and asked for its managers' input on how to proceed. By assuming that the managers would not notice her suppression of the data, she underestimated their competencies and provided misleading results.

Concerning the fee issue, a renegotiation of the originally agreed-upon fees requested by the client was not unreasonable under the circumstances. The psychologist should have cooperated with the client to do all that she could do to rectify the original errors.

Not only were the psychologist's own behavior and professional reputation of ethical concern but also she failed to consider possible attributions that might be made to the profession as a whole. By attempting to cover up her mistakes rather than to address the shortcomings, she possibly left the entire profession in negative repute in the minds of the persons with whom she worked.

D. Case Implications

Students in training should be taught that research does not always turn out as intended. The goal should be to design sound research which tests hypotheses or procedures adequately, not to obtain confirming data. Honest reporting of research results is an ethical imperative, even when the results are not what the researcher or client might wish. The psychologist should also avoid creating false impressions (e.g., the idea that the results are statistically or practically important when in fact they are not, or when they reflect only selected parts of the overall findings).

Clients similarly need to know at the beginning of a project what psychologists can and cannot reasonably assure in their delivery of research services. There are no absolute assurances that research will come out a particular way; if so, there would be little point in conducting a study. Clients do not need or expect absolute guarantees of outcomes. Rather, they need to know what the relevant research issues are and the various possible alternative outcomes that might occur. On that basis they can make informed and appropriate decisions on how to proceed.

All professionals make mistakes from time to time and may discover midway into projects unanticipated problems. Professional integrity mandates acknowledging errors and correcting them as quickly and painlessly as possible.

Case 30

Recording Data Without Consent

A. Statement of the Problem

An I/O psychologist who managed the employee survey research program for a large organization was conducting a research project consisting of focus groups convened to discuss the results of a survey and to solicit feedback on the survey program. After the first few groups expressed considerable dissatisfaction with senior management, the psychologist decided to audiotape the discussions so that he would have all of the facts and impressions verbatim and could be complete and accurate in quotations included in the presentation to be made to senior management.

Because he had no intentions of sharing the recordings with anyone else, the psychologist did not obtain informed consent of the participants being taped. In fact, he did not even make the participants aware of the recording device, hiding the tape-recording device from overt view. During the presentation to senior management, the existence of the tapes was discovered, and the CEO asked to listen to them. The psychologist indicated that he would not be able to share the tapes with anyone because the participants had not been informed in advance that the tapes might be used in this way and because he would therefore be behaving unprofessionally and unethically. The CEO acquiesced to this decision but expressed concern about the psychologist's judgment. The psychologist then destroyed the tapes to assure their inaccessibility.

B. Ethics Code Standards

Ethical Standard 5.01 Discussing the Limits of Confidentiality

(c) Permission for electronic recording of interviews is secured from clients. . . .

Ethical Standard 5.02 Maintaining Confidentiality

Psychologists have a primary obligation and take reasonable precautions to respect the confidentiality rights of those with whom they work or consult, recognizing that confidentiality

may be established by law, institutional rules, or professional or scientific relationships.

Ethical Standard 6.13   Informed Consent in Research Filming or Recording

Psychologists obtain informed consent from research participants prior to filming or recording them in any form, unless the research involves simply naturalistic observations in public places and it is not anticipated that the recording will be used in a manner that could cause personal identification or harm.

C. Case Interpretation

Regardless of the psychologist's intentions or response to the CEO's request, or the ethicality of destroying the tapes once they were made, the psychologist erred by recording the focus groups without the knowledge and consent of the participants. Even though the psychologist appropriately denied the CEO's request (since honoring the request would violate additional principles), the potential damage had already been done. Since there could also have been legal implications for the company as a result of the secret recording, the psychologist inappropriately and needlessly placed himself and his employer potentially in harm's way. The same issues apply to modified requests for the taped material, such as written transcripts of the tapes (whether identifying specific respondents or not), since the transcripts would also contain material obtained without informed consent.

D. Case Implications

It can be perfectly legitimate for a psychologist to audiotape or videotape as part of data collection efforts so long as participants give their informed consent and are provided the opportunity not to participate in the process and provided that the psychologist has made arrangements for the proper storage and disposition of the recordings or any derivative items (such as transcripts of the tapes). Psychologists generally need to collect recorded information using means which are not deceptive or inappropriately intrusive. When they do err or commit ethical breaches, they need to attempt to correct the consequences of their behavior and to minimize the risk of its further harm.

Case 31

Misuse of Data Obtained Through a Consulting Engagement

A. Statement of the Problem

An I/O psychologist's consulting firm was engaged by a consortium of companies to develop a set of proprietary selection tests for customer service representative jobs. The project made use of a criterion-related validation strategy. The psychologist anticipated, based on her experience with prior, similar projects, that a high percentage of the initial pool of test items would drop out after preliminary empirical data collection efforts.

To compensate for the inevitable item fallout, the psychologist directed her staff to draft twice as many trial items as would normally be called for. To her surprise, the item analysis conducted after the validation data were collected showed a large percentage of the items to be working very well. In fact, so many of the items had excellent psychometric characteristics that there were enough good ones left over to compose a complete additional test. The consulting firm delivered the validated tests to the client as contracted, and the client was satisfied with the results.

A few months later, the psychologist had her consulting firm assemble another customer service test, using the remaining items and validation data from the prior project. Without the knowledge or permission of the original client, she began efforts to market the new test through a test publisher. The new measure primarily used the empirical data from her work with the client organization.

B. Ethics Code Standards

Ethical Standard 1.15   Misuse of Psychologists' Influence

Because psychologists' scientific and professional judgments and actions may affect the lives of others, they are alert to and guard against personal, financial, social, organizational, or political factors that might lead to misuse of their influence.

Ethical Standard 1.19   Exploitative Relationships

(a) Psychologists do not exploit persons over whom they have ... authority such as ... research participants, and clients....

Ethical Standard 1.25   Fees and Financial Arrangements

(a) As early as is feasible in a professional or scientific relationship, the psychologist and the ... client ... reach an agreement specifying the compensation and the billing arrangements.
(b) Psychologists do not exploit recipients of services or payors with respect to fees.

Ethical Standard 2.03   Test Construction

Psychologists who develop and conduct research with tests and other assessment techniques use scientific procedures and current professional knowledge for test design, standardization, validation, reduction or elimination of bias, and recommendations for use.

Ethical Standard 6.06   Planning Research

(a) Psychologists design, conduct, and report research in accordance with recognized standards of scientific competence and ethical research.

Ethical Standard 6.10   Research Responsibilities

Prior to conducting research ... psychologists enter into an agreement with participants that clarifies the nature of the research and the responsibilities of each party.

C. Case Interpretation

This case raises several complex and somewhat ambiguous issues. The fact that the psychologist's firm delivered everything it had promised to the client consortium does not address all the ethical issues of this case.

To the psychologist's credit, there was apparently no premeditated attempt to exploit the situation for her own gain. Indeed, it was the psychologist's intent to conduct thorough and professional work on behalf of the client that created the extra items in question. Still, the ownership of the unused test may appropriately be questioned.

Since the psychologist competently performed all the contracted duties, it might be argued that any remaining usable items belonged to her. There are limitations to this argument. Although it was the psychologist's and her firm's time and resources that were invested in developing the large number of test items, the client also had an investment in creating the items. The developmental costs of all items, not just those used in the final test, were presumably covered by the contracted consulting fee. There was time invested by the client company's employees in evaluating the much larger than normal trial set of test items in the validation data collection effort.

It might also be argued that since the test marketed by the psychologist was an unexpected offshoot of the test development effort and since the psychologist did not intentionally exploit the resources of the firm, no harm was done by her subsequent use of those items. The psychologist erred, however, in not recognizing the potential proprietary rights of her organizational client and in not addressing the issue as soon as it arose. Even if it was not within the realm of reasonable possibility to have anticipated the issue of the leftover test items, when that result became clear, and the opportunity to publish the test potentially presented itself, the psychologist should have contacted the original client, explained the situation, and sought permission for her publishing plan.

There is also a technical issue in this case. To market a test on the basis of the original sample alone raises concerns about the adequacy of the validation of the test when it was being offered for use with populations other than the originally intended one. Further research with other samples would not only have improved the technical data base for the test but might also have helped to make the ownership issues of the test clearer.

D. Case Implications

It is not unusual for consulting psychologists to arrange test development agreements with client companies that explicitly call for the development of more than one test, one of which is retained by the client and the other by the consultant. Or the consultant may, with the prior consent of the client, retain copyright to the tests but give the client rights to use them for specified purposes at reduced or no cost in exchange for their participation in the validation study or for the agreed-upon purposes.

It is the psychologist's responsibility to make clear in advance of research or consulting projects the ownership of tests or other products that are developed as part of contractual work with organizational clients. When, as the result of unanticipated circumstances, commercially marketable products arise from a research or consulting effort, it is the psychologist's responsibility then to clarify the ownership issues before making a decision as to how ethically to proceed.

Case 32 _____

Avoiding Dual Relationships

A. Statement of the Problem

A company employed an I/O psychologist whose normal duties included working directly and individually with supervisors who were having performance management problems with specific employees. Occasionally, supervisors asked the psychologist to work informally with an employee. The psychologist had some success with these referrals, especially in the area of coaching and stress management.

As the number of consulting opportunities with employees grew, the psychologist started what became a thriving side business conducting stress reduction workshops and executive coaching out of his home office. In this work, the psychologist encouraged individual participants to discuss their personal problems and concerns, which often were not job related. These services were generally paid for by the company. In a few cases individuals paid for the services themselves.

The psychologist continued to work with supervisors and individual employees at the company, making a point (in a low-key, but clearly communicated manner) to let his contacts know of the availability of his outside services. When the psychologist considered an individual employee's concerns appropriate for more extended individual work, he encouraged the supervisors to refer their employees who had relevant concerns. In time the side business was large enough that he was able to open an office outside the home and hire support personnel.

The psychologist felt that the outside contacts helped him be more effective in his primary paid employment with the company. He gained insight into problems employees were having that were not necessarily work related. On a very selective basis, the psychologist then shared these insights with the employees' supervisors so that the supervisor could better manage the individual on a day-to-day basis. No permission was obtained for this sharing of information.

B. Ethics Code Standards

Ethical Standard 1.04   Boundaries of Competence

(a) Psychologists provide services ... only within the bound-

aries of their competence, based on their education, training, supervised experience, or appropriate professional experience.

Ethical Standard 1.17   Multiple Relationships

(a) . . . Psychologists must always be sensitive to the potential harmful effects of other contacts on their work and on those persons with whom they deal. A psychologist refrains from entering into or promising another personal, scientific, professional, financial, or other relationship with such persons if it appears likely that such a relationship reasonably might impair the psychologist's objectivity or otherwise interfere with the psychologist's effectively performing his or her functions as a psychologist, or might harm or exploit the other party.

Ethical Standard 1.19   Exploitative Relationships

(a) Psychologists do not exploit persons over whom they have . . . authority such as . . . clients. . . .

Ethical Standard 1.21   Third-Party Requests for Services

(a) When a psychologist agrees to provide services to a person or entity at the request of a third party, the psychologist clarifies to the extent feasible, at the outset of the service, the nature of the relationship with each party. This clarification includes the role of the psychologist . . . , the probable uses of the services provided or the information obtained, and the fact that there may be limits to confidentiality.
(b) If there is a foreseeable risk of the psychologist's being called upon to perform conflicting roles because of the involvement of a third party, the psychologist clarifies the nature and direction of his or her responsibilities, keeps all parties appropriately informed as matters develop, and resolves the situation in accordance with this Ethics Code.

Ethical Standard 5.02   Maintaining Confidentiality

Psychologists have a primary obligation and take reasonable precautions to respect the confidentiality rights of those with whom they work or consult, recognizing that confidentiality may be established by law, institutional rules, or professional or scientific relationships.

C. Case Interpretation

Without obtaining explicit permission of the parties involved, and without attending to the conflicts of interest inherent in the relationships he was establishing, the psychologist in this case created dual relationships with an organizational client and individual employees who worked for that organization. He compounded the initial problems by violating confidentiality of the individual clients. The conflicting and potentially self-serving nature of the psychologist's recommendations for referrals apparently went unrecognized by both the psychologist and managers in the client organization.

The described behavior was unethical from a number of perspectives. First, the psychologist's primary client, the organization, was potentially being exploited by serving as a vehicle for channeling persons into individual services. This arrangement created dual or multiple relationships, the effect of which was to confuse the definition of the client and potentially to cloud objectivity in making specific recommendations. Additionally, using the information obtained in the individual work in consulting with persons in the organization, and vice versa, required the consent of the individual clients. No consent was obtained. Confidentiality was therefore also potentially being violated.

There are also competency questions raised by this case. The psychologist's expertise and training in areas relevant for performing individual services are unclear. To the extent he was providing individual assessment and counseling services, careful attention would be required to assure that the boundaries of competence were not being crossed. Additional training might well have been needed before undertaking such responsibilities.

D. Case Implications

While some dual relationships (such as sexually exploitative ones) are obviously and egregiously wrong, others, more subtle and difficult to detect, may create conditions no less problematic. Dual relationships, while not per se unethical, create considerable opportunity for conflict and exploitation and are best avoided. At the least, they need to be identified and ethically managed. Such relationships need not actually be destructive to the parties involved to be a problem or to create a perception of difficulties.

Psychologists need to be trained to recognize any potential dual relationship situation that may be present. They need to learn to recognize possible dual relationships of both the obvious and more subtle kinds. When a conflict or potential conflict exists, discussing such situations with trusted colleagues may help bring the issues into sharper focus and to assure that potential conflicts do not become actual ones.

Case 33

Pressures to Implement
Psychological Programs Too Soon

A. Statement of the Problem

A medium-size sales-oriented service company was experiencing a high failure rate among its sales personnel. The low sales and high turnover were cause for considerable alarm and focused much of top management's attention.

To help address these concerns, the company's psychologist conducted a literature review and then designed a pilot training program that included a combination of self-diagnostics and self-development efforts that were keyed to the diagnostics. The program was designed to be used in conjunction with the instructor-led courses already in place. This program was introduced on a trial basis in one region and received enthusiastic feedback. There was some, but limited, evidence that the sales failure rates had been modestly reduced by the program. However, the psychologist was concerned that the initial results being attributed to the program may have been due to the regional sales manager's enthusiastic support.

On learning of the success being attributed to the new program, the company's sales vice president stated that the program should immediately be implemented companywide. The psychologist opposed this step as being premature. Instead, he strongly recommended that a larger study of the program be undertaken, including the use of a control group. In addition to the costs involved, the psychologist was also concerned about the possibility that the program might not prove effective on a larger scale, particularly when other factors might have contributed to the initial success. He was also concerned that the program might consume significant amounts of time of new sales trainees at an especially sensitive time in the participants' careers.

The sales vice president was incensed by the psychologist's resistance. He accused the psychologist of being unprofessional and unrealistic by withholding a technique that had proved its relevance for solving a serious business problem. After receiving a vague promise to conduct follow-up research on the program, the psychologist agreed to implement the program companywide.

B. Ethics Code Standards

Ethical Standard 1.14   Avoiding Harm

Psychologists take reasonable steps to avoid harming ... their clients ... and others with whom they work, and to minimize harm where it is foreseeable and unavoidable.

Ethical Standard 6.06   Planning Research

(b) Psychologists plan their research so as to minimize the possibility that results will be misleading.

Ethical Standard 6.07   Responsibility

(a) Psychologists conduct research competently and with due concern for the dignity and welfare of the participants.

Ethical Standard 8.03   Conflicts Between Ethics and Organizational Demands

If the demands of an organization with which psychologists are affiliated conflict with this Ethics Code, psychologists clarify the nature of the conflict, make known their commitment to the Ethics Code, and to the extent feasible, seek to resolve the conflict in a way that permits the fullest adherence to the Ethics Code.

C. Case Interpretation

The psychologist in this case was conflicted because the results of the pilot study were not conclusive, yet he was being placed under strong pressure to implement the training program without any additional evaluation or study. The choice was between implementing a program with possible benefits to the organization and individual employees, but which might also fail, and attempting to continue evaluating the program to determine whether it was worthy of more widespread implementation.

Part of the problems raised by the case might possibly have been prevented by having worked through the research parameters of the pilot program at its outset. When a commitment has been made to evaluate an applied organizational program, it is especially important in planning the evaluation to assure that the program will be protected from undue influence or premature termination. That appears not to have happened in this case.

There are also questions of research design. A pilot program might reasonably have been developed without a control group if the goal was just to work out the details of a program that would later be evaluated more rigorously. In that case, identifying and obtaining approval for a broader plan might help to protect the plan from inappropriate meddling.

The ethicality of proceeding with this program when it is of unknown efficacy depend in part on the program's potential for harm to the participants and to the company. The training program might be judged likely to do little harm to participants (although it may also not help them). The potential harm to the company is in spending money on a program which may be of no or limited value. The participants' lost productivity while attending the program should also be considered. The potential harm to the psychologist is that the program will fail and psychology (and he in particular) will be blamed for the failure.

Of course many training programs are neither designed nor administered by psychologists and receive little or no evaluation as to their effectiveness. When a psychologist is involved, however, he or she has the ethical obligation to attempt to implement programs of known efficacy or to assure that proper evaluation determines the effectiveness of new programs. In instances in which organizational leaders wish to make a decision against the advice of the psychologist, it is important that the consequences and risks of the actions be clearly identified.

In this case, when it became clear that the sales vice president was likely to proceed with the program regardless of other recommendations, the psychologist attempted to make his objections known. He might have done more, however, to get a specific commitment for the plan to evaluate the program and might have attempted, as a compromise, to obtain a budget for evaluating at least some of the programs using a proper research design.

D. Case Implications

The pressure to accelerate the implementation of apparently successful programs or products can be intense, especially in highly competitive, results-oriented corporate environments. Psychologists need to understand that environment, and its intense pressures to produce demonstrable results quickly, if they are to work effectively within it.

Of course clear expectations can go a long way to avoid many conflicts and can better guide the resolution of the conflicts that do occur. By assuming an educational role especially when the pressure is less intense, and in the planning stages of projects, psychologists can lay groundwork for behaving ethically in times of stress or crisis. Managers may by these efforts learn that a well-designed study protected from undue influence may result in a more effective final outcome than one that is rushed prematurely into practice.

Still, there are times when there are legitimate differences of opinion on when it is appropriate to administer even properly evaluated programs. It is the nature of behavioral research that even the best conclusions from research result in probabilities, not absolutes. In resolving differences of opinion on readiness to implement, psychologists need to balance the potential loss to the organization of not taking or delaying action against the potential harm of taking actions prematurely. Whatever resolutions are made of specific situations, psychologists need to help organizations learn from the experience so that inappropriate decision processes are not repeated.

Case 34 _____

Confidentiality of Employee
Assistance Program Referrals

A. Statement of the Problem

An I/O psychologist employed by a large financial organization was asked by the company's chief operations officer (COO) to develop and implement a screening program to identify managers and managerial candidates experiencing drug and alcohol problems. The psychologist's present job duties included responsibility for all management evaluation and training programs.

The COO was concerned about substance abuse after several high-level managers had been asked to resign from the company after performance declines and faulty decisions were found to be linked to their addiction problems. The COO was determined to find and remove any managers who were likely to create problems attributable to substance abuse.

The I/O psychologist suggested to the COO that a more constructive response would be for the organization to implement a referral program for the treatment of employees needing help in recovering from alcohol or drug addiction problems. The COO assigned the I/O psychologist the task of implementing such a system, adding that he remained determined to prevent individuals' emotional health problems from interfering with the future success of the company.

The I/O psychologist worked closely with the company's benefits department to implement an employee assistance program (EAP) targeted to the company's managers. A needs assessment survey found that the company's managers were primarily concerned about the issue of anonymity for participants. Most indicated that they would not participate in such a program if senior management were to be told they had entered the program. The I/O psychologist therefore recommended that employees using the program who missed work due to their treatment be reported as being absent due to illness but not specifically identified as being in the EAP.

Although she had no training or experience in employee or personal counseling, the I/O psychologist was somewhat knowledgeable about EAPs and had worked closely with the program's staff to help operationalize it.

She also continued some involvement with the program's management once it was under way. As a result of her ongoing role, she often had information about who was utilizing the program. She had also spoken at some length with individual managers about their participating in the program when she felt it was needed.

Six months after the EAP was implemented, the I/O psychologist was asked to evaluate a group of candidates for an executive vice president position in the company's retail division. The position was to be a key one, reporting directly to the COO. After a series of assessments, one candidate emerged as the most qualified. When the COO approached the I/O psychologist to express his support for the candidate, she was confronted with a dilemma. She was aware that the favored candidate had recently entered a substance abuse treatment program on referral from the EAP and that the circumstances leading to the candidate's participation in the program had suggested a serious problem. Knowing the COO's concern about the issue, the psychologist shared her knowledge of the candidate's situation with him, noting that the information was to be treated as highly confidential. The candidate was not offered the job, and the COO eventually had him transferred to another division. There was no leakage of the privately transmitted information.

B. Ethics Code Standards

Ethical Standard 1.04   Boundaries of Competence

(a) Psychologists provide services, teach, and conduct research only within the boundaries of their competence, based on their education, training, supervised experience, or appropriate professional experience.
(b) Psychologists provide services ... in new areas or involving new techniques only after first undertaking appropriate study, training, supervision, and/or consultation from persons who are competent in those areas or techniques.

Ethical Standard 1.14   Avoiding Harm

Psychologists take reasonable steps to avoid harming their patients or clients, research participants, students, and others with whom they work, and to minimize harm where it is foreseeable and unavoidable.

Ethical Standard 8.03   Conflicts Between Ethics and Organizational Demands

If the demands of an organization with which psychologists are affiliated conflict with this Ethics Code, psychologists clarify the nature of the conflict, make known their commitment to the Ethics Code, and to the extent feasible, seek to

resolve the conflict in a way that permits the fullest adherence to the Ethics Code.

C. Case Interpretation

A central ethical issue in this case was the I/O psychologist's conflicting roles in the company. The psychologist's serving as an advisor to management was in conflict with her role in the EAP program. By mixing these functions, she compromised the anonymity of a participant in an EAP program which had specifically been established as a confidential one. The roles she allowed herself to assume were inherently conflictual and should not have been merged.

If it were important for the company's management to know that executives were receiving treatment for serious problems affecting their work, then the EAP program would have had to be set up that way at its outset and the operating parameters clearly communicated to the potential participants in the program. Even under these circumstances, the dual roles would be a problem. It was also important to assure that information about program utilization did not inadvertently violate the mandates of the Americans with Disabilities Act as it relates to certain protected conditions.

Still another issue concerns the competence of the I/O psychologist to help set up and help to manage an EAP. The facts of this case suggest that the I/O psychologist was not sufficiently trained either to develop or to implement such a program. Under these circumstances her role at most should have been one of serving as a managerial advisor of the work and appropriate expertise sought elsewhere. Especially problematic was the psychologist's decision to allow herself a role in the ongoing operation of the program. Because she was in a position to work with individual executives and to advise top management on their development, she should have declined any opportunity to become an active participant in the program once it was operationalized.

Under the terms of the program as here defined, unless there was some legal requirement to do otherwise, there was no ethical choice for the psychologist but to refrain from sharing the information she had about the individual's involvement in the substance abuse treatment program. If she had ongoing contact with the EAP client, she might have discussed the dilemma with him and asked for his permission to discuss his situation with the COO. Without such consent, however, the information would have to remain confidential, as the program stipulated.

D. Case Implications

It is not unusual for psychologists employed in private industry to find that job responsibilities are not clearly defined. Since managerial expectations and requirements may differ from psychological ones, it is the psychologist's ethical duty to establish parameters of competence in the organizational context and to assure that job responsibilities are not assumed that are outside the realm of professional expertise.

Since managers cannot be assumed to know the ethical parameters under which psychologists are expected to operate, it is the psychologist's job, not the manager's, to assure compliance with ethical standards. It is also the psychologist's duty to be aware of potential ethical conflicts and to refrain from undertaking assignments that create role conflicts.

Part IV

Research and Academic Issues

Case 35 _____

Research Responsibilities

A. Statement of the Problem

A graduate student collected survey material on the effects of employee benefits on job satisfaction as part of his doctoral dissertation. The literature review extended beyond the dissertation subject to include other areas such as total compensation and satisfaction.

Because of the nature of the literature collected, the student and his doctoral advisor considered the possibility of extending the research to conduct meta-analyses on data which were not pertinent to the dissertation. Since neither of these individuals were experienced in conducting this type of analysis, they invited a faculty member from another university to participate in the research and to advise them on methodological and analytical issues. In return, this outside faculty member would be a coauthor for publications and presentations based on these projects.

A written agreement was drafted by the professors and shown to the graduate student. It specified the number of papers that would be coauthored, the subject of each manuscript, the responsibility of each of the participants for each project, and the order of authorship for each paper. The professors were clear and precise in drafting the contract. The graduate student voiced no concerns at that time and signed the agreement along with the professors.

At the time the student graduated, the first two papers were published and presented as the agreement specified. However, after the student began an academic position, he independently submitted manuscripts based on data that were collected as part of the joint research project. When the other two researchers learned of this behavior and protested, the student responded by filing a complaint with a relevant ethics committee. He claimed that (a) the papers he published and presented were based primarily on the analyses and data from his dissertation and (b) he had been forced into an "unfair agreement" by the seniority and the power the two professors wielded over him as a graduate student. On this basis, he stated that he considered the publication agreement not to be binding on him and asked that the two professors be disciplined.

B. Ethics Code Standards

Ethical Standard 1.19   Exploitative Relationships

(a) Psychologists do not exploit persons over whom they have supervisory, evaluative, or other authority such as students....

Ethical Standard 6.23   Publication Credit

(a) Psychologists take responsibility and credit, including authorship credit, only for work they have actually performed or to which they have contributed.
(b) Principal authorship and other publication credits accurately reflect the relative scientific or professional contributions of the individuals involved, regardless of their relative status. Mere possession of an institutional position, such as Department Chair, does not justify authorship credit. Minor contributions to the research or to the writing for publications are appropriately acknowledged, such as in footnotes or in an introductory statement.
(c) A student is usually listed as principal author on any multiple-authored article that is substantially based on the student's dissertation or thesis.

Ethical Standard 8.07   Improper Complaints

Psychologists do not file or encourage the filing of ethics complaints that are frivolous and are intended to harm the respondent rather than to protect the public.

C. Case Interpretation

The three researchers had agreed in writing on the respective contributions each would make to the various projects and the recognition they would receive on any publications and presentations. It was inappropriate for the student unilaterally to make a decision not to keep his commitment to the other two researchers and, with no word to the other two, not to follow the agreement he had signed. Possibly the professors could have been more proactive in ensuring at the time of the original agreement that the student did not feel intimidated or treated unfairly and that he had been given the opportunity to be an active participant in the drafting of the contract. However, if the student thought that the two professors were exploiting him, it was his obligation at the time of the proposed agreement to voice his concerns and propose alternative terms. Alternatively, when he later wanted to renegotiate the terms, or came to realize that he felt exploited by the original agreement, he should first have contacted the other researchers and attempted to renegotiate the terms. His unilateral behavior in publishing the studies suggested inappropriate behavior.

Concerning the filing of ethics charges against his former professor and colleague, such a decision is not to be made lightly or as part of a preemptive strategy for defending one's position. The costs in time, income, and professional reputation of ethics charges can be considerable, even when the ultimate outcome is decided in favor of the persons complained against. Accusations of unethical behavior filed by a psychologist against another psychologist must not be filed improperly or for self-serving reasons. When, in this case, the now-graduated psychologist was contacted with the concerns about his actions, he needed to have attempted to work through the issues with them and to resolve the dispute or change his own behavior. Ethics charges would, in these circumstances, be a last, not a first, step.

D. Case Implications

Professors are obligated not to mistreat their students, but students and former students also have obligations to behave responsibly. When committing themselves to agreements, regardless of professional position and rank, psychologists, students, and former students should not subsequently unilaterally redefine the terms of previously made agreements simply because their professional status has changed.

Certainly psychologists have obligations not to exploit individuals, especially those over whom they have supervisory or teaching authority. However, it is also inappropriate for an individual to use his/her subordinate status in order to claim, without justification, abuse and manipulation.

When disputes do arise among psychologists, it is almost always better to attempt first to resolve them directly. Only when these means have been exhausted should other alternatives be considered.

Case 36 _____

The Ethics of Reviewing and of Being Reviewed

A. Statement of the Problem

An I/O psychologist submitted an article to a professional journal for publication. On the basis of peer reviews, the journal's editor rejected the article. The author then submitted the same article to a second professional journal. The editor of the second journal recognized the article immediately because she had been one of the reviewers of the article for the first journal and had recommended that the article be rejected.

The policy of the second journal was to provide its own, independent review of each article submitted, regardless of any reviews that may have been made by other journals. However, rather than coordinate the review herself, the editor referred the article to another I/O psychologist to assign reviewers and to serve as the acting editor. The editor did not inform the associate editor of the reasons for the assignment, so that the review would not a priori be prejudiced by the knowledge that the article had previously been rejected. The editor noted to the associate editor that she would accept any publication decision made by the acting editor.

B. Ethics Code Standards

Ethical Standard 1.15   Misuse of Psychologists' Influence

Because psychologists' scientific and professional judgments and actions may affect the lives of others, they are alert to and guard against personal, financial, social, organizational, or political factors that might lead to misuse of their influence.

Ethical Standard 1.17   Multiple Relationships

(b) Likewise, whenever feasible, a psychologist refrains from taking on professional or scientific obligations when preexisting relationships would create a risk of such harm.

C. Case Interpretation

The editor's actions provided a model of ethically appropriate behavior. The fact that an article is rejected by one professional journal does not necessarily mean that it is unworthy of publication or that the article would not be of interest to other journals. High-quality, scientifically rigorous journals each have somewhat different specific values and publication needs. An article rejected by one journal may appropriately be published by another. Still, there may be prejudice, if only unconscious, in the review of an article that is known to have previously been rejected before making its way to another journal. Caution is therefore appropriate.

Although the editor could have tried to be objective and to handle the article herself in the usual manner of reviews, her approach removed any cloud of doubt that the review was contaminated by the prior review experience. She recognized that her judgment was possibly biased (or might give that impression) after having previously recommended rejecting the article for another journal. Thus, the editor appropriately delegated the review to an acting editor who had no knowledge of the first review or outcome. In this manner, the editor helped to assure that the article would receive a fresh review.

D. Case Implications

Editors of professional journals have a serious professional duty to provide a competent and fair evaluation of each article submitted for publication. Their decisions affect not just the scientific knowledge database but also the careers and personal lives of those psychologists who submit articles to journals. Editors have broad, and rather unsupervised, powers to carry out their duties and must be extremely conscious of acting responsibly. It is particularly important for editors to avoid conflicts of interest, or even the appearance of conflicts of interest, in order to maintain the integrity and credibility of professional journals.

Decisions to reject articles are rarely received with emotional quiescence by potential contributors to journals. Even when sound and scientifically necessary criticisms need to be made by reviewers, care must be taken to protect the review process from unintended prejudice and to protect the self-esteem of those whose work is being critiqued or rejected. Providing meaningful and constructive feedback is a skill needed by all of those involved with editing and reviewing journal submissions.

Authors whose work is rejected also have ethical and professional obligations. When their work is rejected, authors should carefully consider the criticisms of their work (which, when properly and attentively executed, have often required considerable unreimbursed time of other, often-prominent professionals). Before resubmitting their work to another journal, authors need to assure that they have attended to the feedback and made constructive use of the correctable objections raised by the reviewers. Scientific and professional writing contributions are, in principle (if too seldom in practice), created for posterity and therefore deserve the best contributions that psychologists are capable of providing.

Case 37 ⎯⎯⎯⎯⎯⎯⎯⎯⎯⎯⎯⎯⎯⎯⎯⎯

Honoring Agreements in Data Collection and Usage

A. Statement of the Problem

An I/O psychologist managed a multirater assessment process for his employer. In this program, supervisors and their superiors received anonymous feedback from the supervisors' subordinates and peers. The data from the feedback were used for purposes both of development and appraisal.

After the program had been implemented, the supervisors being rated complained about the process. They expressed concern about the validity of the ratings. Disgruntled workers in some instances seemed to be using the ratings as an opportunity for retribution. Others, apparently seeking to curry the favor of the persons rated, appeared to be giving artificially high ratings.

In response to these concerns, the psychologist decided to implement an "Olympic" scoring system, in which the highest and lowest ratings were automatically discarded and not reported. This policy was applied to the already-collected-data but was not communicated to participants. Because of the large number of respondents for each person being rated, few scores changed very much by the procedure of dropping the high and low scores.

B. Ethics Code Standards

Ethical Standard 1.07   Describing the Nature and Results of Psychological Services

(a) When psychologists provide assessment ... or other psychological services to ... a group, or an organization, they provide, using language that is reasonably understandable to the recipient of those services, appropriate information beforehand about the nature of such services and appropriate information later about results and conclusions. (See also Standard 2.09, Explaining Assessment Results.)

Ethical Standard 6.19   Honoring Commitments

Psychologists take reasonable measures to honor all commitments they have made to research participants.

C. Case Interpretation

A number of ethical and technical issues are raised by this case. The use of peer and subordinate ratings for simultaneous purposes of evaluation and development, although not unethical per se, raises concerns. Since the mentality and accuracy of raters may differ when ratings are done for purposes of assessment than when they are done for developmental uses, combining these two goals in a single rating system may adversely affect the ratings' validity and reliability. The uses to which ratings are to be put need to be articulated clearly to those completing the rating forms. A higher standard of reliability and accuracy is needed when job consequences, such as promotions or salary increases, derive from the results of the assessment. There may also be a greater risk of legal action by persons being evaluated under such circumstances. With the help of the psychologist and other advisors, this risk should be clearly and carefully evaluated by the company's management prior to making a decision to proceed with such a program.

The question of whether there was systematic bias in ratings should in this case have been explored on an empirical rather than anecdotal basis. Since the data had already been collected, the psychologist could readily have analyzed the data. Were the ratings across respondents reliable? Were they consistent with supervisory ratings? Data analyses could have helped clarify whether there was an actual or imagined problem needing to be addressed.

Choosing to employ the "Olympic" rating system as a safeguard against rater bias was not necessarily inappropriate. The modified scoring system may have been appropriate both for technical reasons and because it might have eased the anxieties of some of the participants. However, decisions on changing the system should generally be made on the basis of research data supporting the superiority of the alternative technology both to the present system and to alternative possibilities. Such changes should not be made casually since extreme ratings may still be valid and discarding data may deny some employees the right to express their opinions.

Having made the decision to revise the process midstream, the psychologist had no reason to keep the modifications a secret. Participants in employee surveys and related data collection methods, such as multirater feedback systems, appropriately expect that their input will be collected and reported accurately and as promised. In the revised scoring methodology the data collected from many raters would be discarded. Participants could have been informed of the changed parameters. Should the process be used again, the revised rating scheme should be made clear to all those involved at the outset of the process.

D. Case Implications

Psychologists choosing to employ multiple ratings of job performance or personal attributes have obligations both to persons being rated and to raters. The requirement of validity and reliability provides protection to those being evaluated. Still, those participating in such rating processes have a right to expect that the system will be implemented as promised. Once such a system has been put into place, psychologists should make every reasonable effort to capture and report accurately participants' input as agreed. When the psychologist's obligations to raters and to persons being rated are in conflict, the psychologist attempts to resolve the conflicts in a way which minimizes harm to all affected parties. As important, conflicts and potential consequences should be anticipated in advance of program implementation, helping to minimize later difficulties.

Case 38

Use of Copyrighted Material in New Instrumentation

A. Statement of the Problem

An I/O psychologist in private organizational consulting practice developed a biodata form for use with his client organizations in selection. Other instruments were commercially available for this purpose, but the psychologist chose not to use them, preferring to create his own instrumentation.

The consultant reviewed the existing literature and job analysis instruments. He then created a pastiche of the various approaches, borrowing liberally from the existing measures. His instrument, which carried a copyright notice in the name of his company, embodied significant features and numerous items from well-known and widely used copyrighted instruments. He did not obtain permission from the copyright holder to use any of the borrowed material, nor was credit given to the original source. He reasoned that since it was only for use in his practice and not being offered for sale to other consultants, such permission was unnecessary.

B. Ethics Code Standards

Ethical Standard 2.02   Competence and Appropriate Use of Assessments and Interventions

(b) Psychologists refrain from misuse of assessment techniques, interventions, results, and interpretations and take reasonable steps to prevent others from misusing the information these techniques provide....

Ethical Standard 2.03   Test Construction

Psychologists who develop and conduct research with tests and other assessment techniques use specific procedures and current professional knowledge for test design, standardization, validation, reduction or elimination of bias, and recommendations for use.

Ethical Standard 6.22   Plagiarism

Psychologists do not present substantial portions or elements of another's work or data as their own, even if the other work or data source is cited occasionally.

Ethical Standard 6.23   Publication Credit

(a) Psychologists take responsibility and credit, including authorship credit, only for work they have actually performed or to which they have contributed.

C. Case Interpretation

The psychologist in this case behaved unethically in two major ways. Most obviously, the pirating of items and concepts from other job analytic assessment instruments was contrary both to ethical standards and to copyright law. There are many examples of materials in the I/O field (e.g., performance appraisal forms) which may be quite similar in concept and approach even though they were developed independently. However, when a source is directly used as a conceptual model and especially when actual items are copied without permission, due credit should be given even if the instrument is in the public domain. When, as in this case, the material is protected by copyright, appropriate written permission to reproduce the material must of course be obtained.

A second issue concerns the absence of validity evidence for the instrument the psychologist created. There was no assurance of content or other validity for this particular measure. Whatever validity and reliability information might have been available for the original instruments, there was no assurance that they extended to this new measure. In creating a new assessment tool, even if it was not wrongly composed of the work of others, the psychologist had an ethical obligation to assure validity for the intended assessment task.

D. Case Implications

Psychologists should be made aware, beginning with their graduate student training, of appropriate procedures for using copyrighted material and of acceptable professional practices in making use of the results of the research activities and programs of their professional colleagues. Protecting copyrighted material is a legal as well as ethical obligation of psychologists.

Additionally, all psychologists need to know what constitutes an appropriate standard for using a new test in practice. Tests of any kind need to meet at least minimal standards of validity and reliability before they are applied.

A final point concerns the duty to confront and/or report ethical violations by other psychologists. Any psychologist who learns of a practice of this sort, or who encounters an instrument raising questions of possible copyright violations, has a duty to address the problem with the source or, if that proves ineffective, to report the behavior to appropriate ethics tribunals (see Ethical Standards 8.04 and 8.05).

Case 39

Authorship and
Publication Agreements

A. Statement of the Problem

Two psychologists, one of whom supervised the other, coauthored a book on a highly specific I/O topic. The coauthors agreed at the time that if one or the other was invited to prepare a chapter for another book on the same topic, then that chapter would also be a collaborative effort, regardless of which psychologist received the invitation.

Later in the year of this agreement, an editor of a book of readings in psychology invited only the senior psychologist to write the summary chapter on the topic of joint interest. That psychologist began working on the chapter without involving the original coauthor and without communicating to the coauthor that assistance would not be sought for the chapter. The new chapter drew heavily on the earlier work written jointly by the two authors.

When the chapter appeared, the coauthor contacted her supervisor and asked why he had breached their agreement. He indicated that only he had been asked to write the chapter and that he had not wanted to hurt her feelings by telling her she had not been invited to be a coauthor. He insisted that he had argued valiantly, but ultimately ineffectively, to have her included.

The published article made no acknowledgment of the previous collaboration. The former collaborator asked for a correction to the chapter and that future printings of the chapter acknowledge her contributions.

B. Ethics Code Standards

Ethical Standard 1.14   Avoiding Harm

Psychologists take reasonable steps to avoid harming their patients or clients, research participants, students, and others with whom they work, and to minimize harm when it is foreseeable and unavoidable.

Ethical Standard 6.22   Plagiarism

Psychologists do not present substantial portions or elements of another's work or data as their own, even if the other work or data source is cited occasionally.

Ethical Standard 6.23   Publication Credit

(b) Principal authorship and other publication credits accurately reflect the relative scientific or professional contributions of the individuals involved, regardless of their relative status. Mere possession of an institutional position, such as Department Chair, does not justify authorship credit. Minor contributions to the research or the writing for publications are appropriately acknowledged, such as in footnotes or in an introductory statement.

C. Case Interpretation

The supervising psychologist in this case behaved problematically by not informing the coauthor, a subordinate of his, of the invitation he had received to prepare a summary chapter based on the two authors' original work. In this manner, he did not maintain the terms of the original agreement. By working independently, and without obtaining the consent of his previous coauthor, the psychologist in this case potentially caused harm to his former collaborator. He also potentially plagiarized his subordinate's work. While in retrospect the inclusiveness of the original agreement might have seemed impractical, and perhaps the agreement should have been reduced to writing, its terms were still relevant unless a renegotiation had occurred.

In order to avoid needless harm to his collaborator, the psychologist had a professional obligation either to honor his previous agreement or to attempt to renegotiate it in light of the changed circumstances. There were several other professionally appropriate possibilities that he might have considered. On receiving the invitation, the first psychologist might have insisted that he would only write the chapter with his coauthor, as had been agreed. Editors are usually amenable to such requests, but if this one were not, the psychologist could certainly have refused to write the chapter. Alternatively, he might have approached his original coauthor, explained the situation, and asked for her suggestions on how to proceed.

The psychologist also drew heavily upon the original book in preparing the summary chapter without giving proper credit to his original coauthor. At the least, the colleague's contributions to the original work on which the new chapter was based should have been prominently acknowledged in the chapter. If the work was mostly overlapping with the previous joint publications, then the psychologist's behavior may also have constituted plagiarism. The psychologist therefore needed to take whatever corrective steps he could to restore the original terms of the agreement and to minimize any harm his former colleague may have suffered.

D. Case Implications

Psychologists should recognize their ethical obligations not to harm their colleagues. They generally need to honor their agreements with colleagues in conducting and reporting the results of research. Circumstances can and do change over time in which case it becomes the obligation of all parties to reach new agreements if the previous ones are no longer tenable. Certainly this involves at a minimum keeping colleagues with whom one previously had agreements informed of the new parameters, so that a mutually agreeable revision of the contract can be negotiated. Unilateral decisions in such cases should obviously be avoided.

It is certainly expected at all times that psychologists only take independent publication credit for work that they have actually done on their own. Others who have assisted the author directly and indirectly should be given appropriate acknowledgment.

When, regardless of the fault or intentionality, ethically problematic behavior has occurred, the ethical psychologist accepts responsibility to acknowledge the situation and to correct the ill effects as much and as quickly as possible. Such a course of action will help minimize further damage that would otherwise result from the behavior.

Case 40 _____

Publication Credit

A. Statement of the Problem

An I/O psychology graduate student, along with other I/O graduate students, participated as a member of a research team, supervised by a faculty member of the university's I/O psychology faculty. The research was carried out in an industrial setting.

In publications deriving from this research which appeared in print 3 to 4 years later, the academic psychologist failed to acknowledge the contributions of the graduate students and incorporated results obtained by other members of the research team without giving them any credit. In doing so, the professor assumed full credit for the research.

The research attracted considerable attention and served to enhance the psychologist's professional reputation. However, the research had been the product of a joint effort of several students and the faculty member, and the students' contributions were not even acknowledged. In fact, the other participants had not even consented to or been aware that the material they helped to create was being submitted for publication.

When the students, by then all professional psychologists, learned of the publications, they contacted their former professor. In his customary gracious, if distant and slightly forbidding manner, he indicated that their recollection was inconsistent with his and that in his view their contributions were those typical of rather junior graduate students. Moreover, he noted, they had contributed nothing to the write-up of the article, nor had they asked about being included in any publications from the study.

The students replied that they had not contributed to the writing up of the articles because they had not been asked to do so and that had they been consulted they would have been happy to do their share of the work. They also noted that they had conducted the literature reviews, gathered the data, and done the bulk of the data analyses. Two of them had successfully defended theses based on this research.

The faculty member then stated that he did not concur in their observations and recollections and clearly communicated that the matter was in his mind closed. Dissatisfied with the responses of the faculty member, the psychologists wrote to the editor of the journals in which the publications appeared and to the ethics committee of a national association to which the psychologist belonged and asked for an independent review of the matter.

B. Ethics Code Standards

Ethical Standard 1.19   Exploitative Relationships

(a) Psychologists do not exploit persons over whom they have supervisory, evaluative, or other authority such as students. . . .

Ethical Standard 6.23   Publication Credit

(a) Psychologists take responsibility and credit, including authorship credit, only for work they have actually performed or to which they have contributed.

(b) Principal authorship and other publication credits accurately reflect the relative scientific or professional contributions of the individuals involved, regardless of their relative status. Mere possession of an institutional position, such as Department Chair, does not justify authorship credit. Minor contributions to the research or the writing for publications are appropriately acknowledged, such as in footnotes or in an introductory statement.

(c) A student is usually listed as principal author on any multiple-authored article that is substantially based on the student's dissertation or thesis.

Ethical Standard 8.05   Reporting Ethical Violations

If an apparent ethical violation is not appropriate for informal resolution under Standard 8.04 or is not resolved properly in that fashion, psychologists take further action appropriate to the situation, unless such action conflicts with confidentiality rights in ways that cannot be resolved. Such action might include referral to state or national committees on professional ethics or to state licensing boards.

C. Case Interpretation

In assuming full publication credit for the research, the I/O psychology professor acted in an inappropriate manner. The ownership of the data in this case should have explicitly been clarified at the time of the data gathering, particularly as it related to subsequent publications. Although the psychologist publishing the work certainly deserved appropriate publication credit, so did the others who were a significant part of the original research effort. The fellow researchers' status as students at the time of the research did not remove the obligation to comply with the ethical standards. The persons not credited in this case appropriately took action to confront the unethical behavior and, receiving no satisfaction from their direct dealings with the supervisory faculty member, appropriately took other steps to address the behavior.

D. Case Implications

Psychology faculty perhaps inevitably reside in positions of greater power than their students. They need to avoid exploitative relationships with their students and, at the least, to assure that the terms of a working relationship and the outcome of its products are made explicit at the start of projects. Because the publication process may take years, and because students often lose contact with their parent institutions when they graduate, particularly when they move on to nonacademic positions, there may be temptation to minimize their contributions to a project. After all, it might be reasoned, they were just learning and may not have participated in the write-up of the work.

Assuredly there are circumstances in which no publication credit (other than, perhaps, a footnote) is deserved and in which graduate or undergraduate students overrate their contributions and minimize those of their faculty. Adjudicating after the fact the credit to be assigned to those working on a project would entail examining specific factual information, not just perceptions of contributions. Always it is more difficult for outside parties retrospectively to assign credit and to determine what actually happened than for professionals and professionals in the making to address these issues while the project is ongoing, and particularly before the work is begun.

When specific violations of the ethics code are reasonably believed to have occurred, action must be taken by psychologists with awareness of the behavior at issue. Preferably the contact is first with the allegedly at-error party. When that step cannot be taken, or is inappropriate or ineffective in resolving the matter, there is an ethical obligation to take the matter further and seek its airing and resolution in a relevant forum. Because such steps are consequential, they should never be undertaken without just cause, but when such concern legitimately exists, failure to take action may itself be unethical.

Case 41

Fairness in Book Reviews

A. Statement of the Problem

During her graduate education, an I/O psychologist worked with a respected group of faculty members to develop a model for training in organizations that focused on off-site, brief classroom learning principles. Her dissertation focused on creating and testing an applied training program based on the principles of the model. After several years of publishing many articles and a book on the model, the I/O psychologist became a widely cited expert in the training field.

In time, the I/O psychologist's research interests shifted to job design and motivation. Due to her many other commitments, including those associated with her academic job, she had not read or published in the training field for some time. However, when she was approached at a national conference by an editor to review a book that presented a new training model, she agreed to do the review since she was curious about new developments in her original field of interest. She discovered that the book presented a systems-based model of training which was largely based on a critical response to the original model upon which her earlier work was built. The new model drew on recent literature with which the psychologist was only slightly familiar and a covariance structure model that she did not know at all. Her greatest concern, however, was that the authors did not have an adequate understanding of the earlier theory and were, as a result, arriving at erroneous conclusions.

In the preparation of her book review, the I/O psychologist focused rather energetically on the authors' "lack of historical grounding" and "incomplete presentation." She speculated that the model was an attempt to apply an inappropriate but currently popular set of ideas to the training context and that it would probably be of interest to only a limited audience and for a limited period of time. She did not discuss in any detail the content of the new model or the literature upon which it was based. She made no mention of the covariance structure model or the empirical studies which had demonstrated the effectiveness of the model in applied settings. Because of her previously established reputation in the training field, the review was published and widely read. The book sold modestly and was dropped by the publisher after its initial printing.

B. *Ethics Code Standards*

Ethical Standard 1.05   Maintaining Expertise

Psychologists who engage in ... research ... or other professional activities maintain a reasonable level of awareness of current scientific and professional information in their fields of activity, and undertake ongoing efforts to maintain competence in the skills they use.

Ethical Standard 1.06   Basis for Scientific and Professional Judgments

Psychologists rely on scientifically and professionally derived knowledge when making scientific or professional judgments or when engaging in scholarly or professional endeavors.

C. *Case Interpretation*

This case concerns the professional responsibility of a psychologist and researcher when engaged in the preparation of a published critique of a colleague's work to consider and present objectively all of the evidence which supports or refutes this work. In this case, the reviewer–psychologist did not make sufficient efforts to assure objectivity in a review. Certainly psychologists have a right to hold and express their own professional opinions of the value of other psychologists' work. They also can and should evaluate a work on its judged theoretical and empirical soundness. However, they must always make a reasonable effort to present all available information concerning such work and to do so in an objective manner. Critiques of others' work should be undertaken only where the reviewer has sufficient and up-to-date knowledge of the specific topic to make complete and informed judgments. This is particularly important in controversial areas in which psychologists may reasonably be expected to disagree. Psychologists also must be especially cautious in areas in which the reviewer may have a potential conflict of interest, or even when there reasonably exists the perception of conflicts of interest.

Suppression of competing evidence in a review is analogous to keeping data which conflict with one's desired research outcomes out of a research report; both actions suggest ethical concerns. Moreover, even when reviewers believe that a work has faults, they should not fail to mention its merits as well, both as a service to the reader and out of fairness to the author and publisher.

D. *Case Implications*

Editors soliciting and publishing reviews of psychological works should take steps to assure balanced and objective reviews based on the relevant body of theoretical and empirical material consistent with the authors' purposes in writing. They should make clear to potential psychologist reviewers that self-disqualifications (removing oneself from a review assignment when there are potential conflicts of interest) are appropriate, especially when there is reasonable possibility to question objectivity. When, after such precautions, a review still seems potentially one-sided, or when material is known to be controversial, editors should also consider obtaining additional reviews in order to present all aspects of psychological work.

Case 42

Confidentiality and Objectivity in Reviews

A. *Statement of the Problem*

An I/O psychologist had been serving on the editorial board of a respected testing and measurement journal for a number of years. While reading an article sent to her for blind review, she recognized the work of a graduate student studying with a colleague at another university. The I/O psychologist and her colleague had collaborated on research and writing projects on a number of occasions, and each had been instrumental in advising and helping to place one another's graduate students in their professional jobs.

At a recent conference, the colleagues and their graduate students had spent an evening together, and it was during this meeting that the I/O psychologist had talked at some length with the graduate student about his research. The two had found many common professional interests in their approach to scale development, and the I/O psychologist respected the graduate student's theoretical insight.

In the manuscript submitted by the graduate student, the I/O psychologist was surprised to find significant psychometric problems, including very low reliability coefficients for the scales developed by the graduate student. He selectively cited only the two acceptably high reliability coefficients out of the eight presented, thus implying that the highest coefficients were representative of the entire range of reliability coefficients. The I/O psychologist was disappointed and a little confused about the problems, given her favorable impression of the graduate student's skills, but decided to trust her earlier impressions of his work and review the research more positively than she might otherwise have done. After submitting a generally favorable review of the graduate student's manuscript, the I/O psychologist contacted her colleague and discussed how the graduate student could improve his scales before using them in future research.

B. *Ethics Code Standards*

Ethical Standard 1.17   Multiple Relationships

(a) ... A psychologist refrains from entering into ... another

personal, scientific, professional, financial, or other relationship with such persons if it appears likely that such a relationship reasonably might impair the psychologist's objectivity or otherwise interfere with the psychologist's effectively performing his or her functions as a psychologist, or might harm or exploit the other party.

(b) Likewise, whenever feasible, a psychologist refrains from taking on professional or scientific obligations when preexisting relationships would create a risk of such harm.

Ethical Standard 3.03   Avoidance of False or Deceptive Statements

(a) Psychologists do not make public statements that are false, deceptive, misleading, or fraudulent, either because of what they state, convey, or suggest or because of what they omit, concerning their research, practice, or other work activities or those of persons or organizations with which they are affiliated.

C. Case Interpretation

The author of the review allowed her social contacts with the contributor of the article to affect her objectivity in reviewing the article. Prior knowledge of the contributor's thinking or research should not have influenced the reviewer's analysis of the manuscript she was reviewing. By citing only the highest of the range of reliability coefficients presented in the original sources, the author had made a misleading statement. The statement would be likely to deceive readers because it made only a partial disclosure of the relevant facts regarding the scale. The reviewer had a responsibility to help protect the journal and its readers from such statements.

Additionally, by talking with her colleague about the research, the author violated the confidentiality of the contributor of the article. The graduate student understood when he submitted the article that the journal's review process would be blind and that his work and his identity would be kept confidential.

D. Case Implications

To maintain the credibility of the review process, it is critical that the highest levels of objectivity and confidentiality be maintained. Even when a reviewer may think he or she knows the identity of an author of a manuscript being reviewed, the mind-set needs to be one of distance and dispassion. Only then can appropriate decisions be made about articles and the inevitable defects of work be identified.

Psychologists should strive to be complete in reporting research findings, and they should not suppress information in an effort to bias a review in a positive or negative direction. When they have not done so, it is the reviewer's responsibility to try to identify the problem and assure corrective action or to make a recommendation not to publish. When a reviewer cannot maintain objectivity in reviewing a manuscript as a result of personal relations with the author or other factors that might affect objectivity, the review should not be undertaken. At the least, the potentially biasing prior relationship should be identified to the editor requesting the review. The reviewer must at all times respect the confidentiality of any material reviewed.

Case 43

When Testimony Would Be Compelled

A. Statement of the Problem

A state personnel department contracted with a consulting psychologist to review the department's selection process and to advise the agency on the defensibility and liabilities of its then-current selection processes. The psychologist accepted the assignment, reviewed the appropriate materials, and sent the agency a final report with her recommendations. The report was labeled as being confidential and contained a frank assessment of some of the limitations of the system, including detailed analyses which identified the current adverse impact liabilities. Her analyses identified a number of problems with the current system and strongly recommended immediate changes if the agency wished to minimize its liabilities. With the report, she had fulfilled all the obligations of the contract.

A few months after the report was submitted, the selection process was challenged in Equal Employment Opportunity Commission litigation. The psychologist was contacted by the plaintiff (who had somehow learned of her work with the agency) and asked for a copy of the report. She referred the question to the state agency. The agency's legal advisor denied permission to obtain the report. Although not released by the psychologist, the report was ultimately obtained by the plaintiff from the agency through the discovery process in the legal proceedings.

After obtaining the psychologist's report, whose contents were deemed highly supportive of its case, the plaintiff contacted the psychologist and asked her to testify as one of its paid expert witnesses. The contract with the state agency had not specified any obligation or limitation concerning such matters. Contacts in the state agency indicated that they did not anticipate calling the psychologist as a witness, paid or otherwise. The psychologist declined the invitation to testify for the plaintiff, stating that in her mind it would be ethically inappropriate.

The psychologist was nonetheless subpoenaed by the plaintiff. She was unsuccessful in her attempt to quash the subpoena. On the stand, she attempted to invoke a psychologist–client privilege to prevent her testimony, since she knew that her testimony would be damaging to her former client's case. The judge ruled that because her state did not allow licensure for I/O psychologists, and the confidentiality privilege in that state applied only to licensed psychologists, she could not refuse to testify on the grounds of psychologist–client privilege. She then asked the judge to be exempted from testimony on the grounds that she could only provide testimony as a paid expert witness, that she was in fact not being paid for her services by the plaintiff, and that she could not accept the plaintiff as a client because the defendant was already her client. The judge also disallowed this argument but did insist that the plaintiff pay her for her services at her standard professional rate.

Under these circumstances the psychologist felt she could not refuse to testify and did so, limiting her statements to the factual information in the report and to verifying what she had said in the report. She attempted to mitigate the effects of her testimony by repeatedly noting that her client hired her to correct its problems and that she was testifying against her will. Her testimony proved helpful to the plaintiff's successful litigation.

B. Ethics Code Standards

Ethical Standard 1.02   Relationship of Ethics and Law

If psychologists' ethical responsibilities conflict with law, psychologists make known their commitment to the Ethics Code and take steps to resolve the conflict in a responsible manner.

Ethical Standard 5.01   Discussing the Limits of Confidentiality

Psychologists discuss with persons and organizations with whom they establish a scientific or professional relationship ... (1) the relevant limitations on confidentiality, including limitations where applicable in ... organizational consulting, and (2) the foreseeable uses of the information generated through their services.
(b) Unless it is not feasible or is contraindicated, the discussion of confidentiality occurs at the outset of the relationship and thereafter as new circumstances may warrant.

Ethical Standard 5.02   Maintaining Confidentiality

Psychologists have a primary obligation and take reasonable precautions to respect the confidentiality rights of those with whom they work or consult....

Ethical Standard 5.10   Ownership of Records and Data

Recognizing that ownership of records and data is governed by legal principles, psychologists take reasonable and lawful steps so that records and data remain available to the extent necessary to serve the best interests of ... organizational clients....

C. Case Interpretation

In this case, the psychologist behaved ethically and responsibly in her handling of the challenging issues aroused by the request to testify. Still, there were some preventative measures which may have helped minimize the later threat to the client.

At the outset of the project, the psychologist should have recognized the potential for misuse of the report she was asked to write, particularly in the context of working for a public agency in which no written products can be assumed to be outside ultimate public scrutiny. The initial contract for the consulting engagement in this case proved inadequate to protect the interests of the client. Even when the psychologist cannot anticipate all of the ways that the confidentiality of client information could be at risk, the consultant is expected to engage in discussions with the client about possible limitations on the protection of that information. In this case one of the clearest issues to be discussed should have been the legal limits on confidentiality that apply to materials in the public sector.

D. Case Implications

Psychologists do a disservice to their clients and themselves if they ignore the litigious environment in which the practice of I/O psychology today occurs. There is therefore no single step in both internal and external consulting that is more important than the initial contract. The purpose of the contract is to set out expectations to agree on the deliverable products or services and on fees and schedules for completion of the work. Often overlooked in the rush to finalize the agreement is the anticipation of potential problems and what to do if they occur.

Often consulting psychologists learn which problems to anticipate by unfortunate experience. Since other consultants and professionals may already have had similar experiences, psychologists should seek out senior colleagues to think through issues they may be overlooking. It is always easier, cleaner, and less costly (including to professional reputation) to anticipate and avoid a problem than to address it after it has become one.

Case 44 —————————————

Reporting Back Data From Research Studies

A. Statement of the Problem

A university-based I/O psychologist developed a relationship with the managing director of a large local organization. Because one of the divisions in the firm had some internal problems, the director, at the suggestion of the psychologist, agreed to allow the psychologist and several graduate students to conduct a series of research studies that would benefit the researchers and possibly assist in understanding the nature of the difficulties. No specific agreements were made about information to be provided to the company's officials, but over a 3-year period the results of these studies were reported to the director, who continued to encourage the program of research.

No monetary compensation was requested by the psychologist, and the organization provided no financial support to the students or the psychologist during this time. At the end of the 3-year period, the director requested a comprehensive and detailed report of all research that had been conducted but offered no remuneration. Because of the voluntary nature of the services and other commitments, the psychologist did not feel obligated to provide the report and ended the relationship. No referral was made.

B. Ethics Code Standards

Ethical Standard 1.23   Documentation of Professional and Scientific Work

(a) Psychologists appropriately document their professional and scientific work in order to facilitate provision of services later by them or by other professionals, to ensure accountability, and to meet other requirements of institutions or the law.

Ethical Standard 1.25   Fees and Financial Arrangements

(a) As early as is feasible in a professional ... relationship,

the psychologist and the ... client ... reach an agreement specifying the compensation and the billing arrangements.

Ethical Standard 4.09   Terminating the Professional Relationship

(a) Psychologists do not abandon ... clients.

(c) Prior to termination for whatever reason, except where precluded by the ... client's conduct, the psychologist discusses the ... client's views and needs, provides appropriate pretermination counseling, suggests alternative service providers as appropriate, and takes other reasonable steps to facilitate transfer of responsibility to another provider if the patient or client needs one immediately.

Ethical Standard 5.01   Discussing the Limits of Confidentiality

(a) Psychologists discuss with persons and organizations with whom they establish a ... professional relationship ... the foreseeable uses of the information generated through their services.

C. Case Interpretation

This case points to the need to clarify and establish respective obligations and compensations prior to conducting research. As the project changes scope or direction, a renegotiated agreement is then necessary.

Certainly the psychologist in this case should have made explicit rather than casual, and preferably written, agreements with the firm's director. This was especially important in a project of this duration. This agreement should have specified the use of the data collected, the nature of the reports (if any) to be provided to the director, ownership of the data, confidentiality rights of participants, access to the recommendations of the study, payments or other consideration to be made, and any other pertinent governing parameters.

Although there was no monetary arrangement involved in this case, the relationship with the host organization still constituted a client-consulting one. It did provide benefit to the psychologist and the graduate students in that a field setting was provided to conduct research.

The time provided by the director and the employees of the division also had value. Moreover, the continued reporting of the results of the research studies to the organization's managers created an expectation that this was part of the agreement. Whatever the mutual consideration, there was a professional obligation to clarify in advance the respective roles and obligations of all parties to the project.

The psychologist erred by not making clear to the organizational representatives the mutual rewards and responsibilities to be obtained from the relationship. If the psychologist expected payment for information relating to the results of the studies, this should have been agreed upon in advance. When the client requested work that was considered excessive if it was to be unremunerated, the psychologist had an ethical obligation to terminate the agreement responsibly. Referral to other sources should have been discussed at that time and arrangements made, if necessary, for the psychologist to cooperate with a new provider of services, so that the new work could build on what had already been done.

D. Case Implications

Organizations allowing the use of their personnel and facilities for research studies should be viewed as clients. It is the responsibility of the psychologist, even if direct financial support is not involved, to address at the outset of a study the issue of access to information obtained in the study. The specific form the reported information is to take, and who is to bear the costs of it, should be clarified in advance and agreed upon by all relevant parties. In a psychologist–client relationship extending over many years, it may be necessary to renegotiate the terms of the agreement from time to time. The psychologist should take responsibility for initiating such negotiations where appropriate.

Termination of a professional relationship can happen for many reasons. It is the psychologist's responsibility to assure, to the extent he has the opportunity to do so, that the relationship is ended responsibly. This includes discussion of the reasons for the termination, a review of alternative courses of action if additional services are still needed, and cooperation with new service providers to the extent that their work is ethical and needs to build on what was already done.

Part V

Professional Training and Certification Issues

Case 45

Training Requirements in I/O Psychology

A. Statement of the Problem

A professor in an I/O psychology program at a major university was visited by a graduate student from the school's experimental psychology program. The graduate student was in the final stages of a dissertation that involved learning experiments with hyperphagic rats. The graduate student was appropriately pessimistic about the job market in academia and generally dissatisfied with the career opportunities then available in academic psychology. In thinking about ways in which his experimental training might be applied to industry, the student thought that programs in stress management and interpersonal communication skills would make use of his understanding of learning principles and that test development could make use of his training in statistics. Alternatively, he considered just seeking out a job in I/O psychology directly, since he had heard that industry cared more about what services one could provide than what credentials one possessed. In his meeting with the professor, the student requested the names of people in industry who might provide consulting opportunities, which, hopefully, could lead to paid employment. He asked for suggestions of a book or two he might read to be able to, as he phrased it, "pass himself off" as an I/O psychologist.

Rather than supplying the student with contacts, the professor pointed out the ethical implications of what the student intended to do and informed the student that psychologists must receive adequate training in the area for which they intend to practice. The professor recommended that the student first find out more about the field and, if he had ongoing interest in the field, that he obtain appropriate training should he still want to change his specialization. Since their university did not have relevant training opportunities for the student, the I/O psychologist offered to make inquiries of several I/O colleagues regarding the possibilities of postdoctoral training at their institutions. The professor also helped the student think through other ways in which his training might appropriately be applied to industrial applications.

B. Ethics Code Standards

Ethical Standard 1.04   Boundaries of Competence

(a) Psychologists provide services, teach, and conduct research only within the boundaries of their competence, based on their education, training, supervised experience, or appropriate professional experience.
(b) Psychologists provide services, teach, or conduct research in new areas or involving new techniques only after first undertaking appropriate study, training, supervision, and/or consultation from persons who are competent in those areas or techniques.

Ethical Standard 2.06   Unqualified Persons

Psychologists do not promote the use of psychological assessment techniques by unqualified persons.

C. Case Interpretation

This case concerns the responsibility of psychologists and those who are in training to become psychologists to practice within their areas of competency or to prepare themselves properly for new career directions. Although the Ethics Code technically applies only to members of the professional associations adopting the code (e.g., APA, SIOP), many graduate programs require that their students abide by the Ethics Code, and behavior contrary to the code may be grounds for dismissal or corrective action. Regardless, faculty have an obligation to try to educate students in the ethical practice of psychology and in the applicability of ethics to student behavior. In this case, the student was considering a course of behavior which, though understandable, could have resulted in damage to clients (in that the student was not properly trained in what he proposed to do) and damage to the profession (in that negative attributions might be made to all of I/O psychology from any inappropriate or problematic actions).

The faculty member in this case acted appropriately in two ways. First, he pointed out the ethical problems involved in attempting to practice I/O psychology when all the student's training and experience was in another area of psychology. Second, the psychologist attempted to help the student with his needs by offering to help the student locate suitable training opportunities. This action was consistent with the faculty member's responsibility as a teacher and advisor in a psychology training program.

D. Case Implications

Psychologists-in-training are usually not members of professional associations and typically do not hold licenses which mandate an obligation to abide by psychologists' Ethics Code. Still, many training programs expect and require that students be familiar with and behave consistently with the code. I/O psychology faculty should make clear to the students in their programs and other students with whom they come in contact the limits of professional competence and ways to acquire new areas of competence when, because of personal choice or external necessity, a career redirection is sought.

Persons trained in other areas of psychology may appropriately desire experience or training in I/O psychology. Academic psychologists need to be aware of appropriate educational and training opportunities around the country so they can appropriately advise students with legitimate retraining interests or needs on ethically appropriate ways to obtain the desired training.

Programs also need to make graduate students aware of the ethical parameters governing their behavior, of ways to identify ethical conflicts inherent in proposed courses of action, and of steps they can take to obtain further guidance when ethical ambiguities remain.

Case 46 _____

Practice of I/O Psychology by a Clinical Psychologist

A. Statement of the Problem

A clinical psychologist offered traditional mental health services in his independent practice. As the result of the erosion of his insurance-based practice by managed care plans, he had to make major cutbacks and lay off several of his employees. Since he realized that the mental health market was unlikely to change anytime soon, and in fact would probably get worse, he sought new ways to apply his clinical psychology expertise and still earn his accustomed living in the practice of psychology.

Industrial applications appeared to offer better promise of attractive and fairly rapid financial returns, so he turned his attentions to corporate work. Acting independently, he contacted a business manager colleague of his acquaintance. He was asked to assist the company in its screening of executive candidates. Using the same assessment measures which he had learned in his clinical training (including an intelligence measure and several popularly used objective measures of psychopathology, including the Rorschach), and without benefit of job analysis, the clinical psychologist made sweeping judgments on the candidates' fitness or lack of fit with the executive role. He failed to consider any work performance data or background information. Candidates were either hired or not at least partly based on the psychologist's recommendation.

The manager with whom the psychologist worked found the approach to be very interesting and felt that the psychologist's assessments helped the company learn things about the candidates that would otherwise be unavailable. Since the psychologist liked the work well enough, and the economic rewards seemed much more promising than in mental health, in time he closed his clinical practice and offered only consulting services to business.

The psychologist ultimately developed a large assessment practice. He used the same battery for executive candidates in a variety of positions. With several of his organizational clients, executive candidates would not be hired or promoted until the psychologist had assessed the candidates and given his evaluation. Industrial psychologists in his city knew of his practice and complained to each other but said nothing to the psychologist himself.

B. Ethics Code Standards

Ethical Standard 1.04   Boundaries of Competence

(a) Psychologists provide services ... and conduct research only within the boundaries of their competence, based on their education, training, supervised experience, or appropriate professional experience.

(b) Psychologists provide services ... or conduct research in new areas or involving new techniques only after first undertaking appropriate study, training, supervision, and/or consultation from persons who are competent in those areas or techniques.

(c) In those emerging areas in which generally recognized standards for preparatory training do not yet exist, psychologists nevertheless take reasonable steps to ensure the competence of their work and to protect patients, clients, students, research participants, and others from harm.

Ethical Standard 8.04   Informal Resolution of Ethical Violations

When psychologists believe that there may have been an ethical violation by another psychologist, they attempt to resolve the issue by bringing it to the attention of that individual if an informal resolution appears appropriate....

Ethical Standard 8.05   Reporting Ethical Violations

If an apparent ethical violation is not appropriate for informal resolution under Standard 8.04 ... psychologists take further action appropriate to the situation. ... Such action might include referral to the state or national committees on professional ethics or to state licensing boards.

C. Case Interpretation

In this case the clinical psychologist assumed responsibilities for which prior training and experience had not been obtained and thus behaved contrary to the ethical principles. The potential negative consequences of malpractice to an organization can be as serious as if an I/O psychologist, untrained in such matters, began to counsel individual psychotherapy clients. The fact that organization may not have the competence to assess whether psychologists are properly trained in the specific services they offer does not remove the psychologist's ethical obligations to (a) seek and accept only positions or assignments for which they are qualified; and/or (b) undertake training, supervision, consultation, or other relevant help from other psychologists who have the training and experience in the I/O areas.

By performing assessments without proper job analyses and using psychological instruments with questionable validity for the purposes for which they were used, the psychologist also placed his organizational clients and the individual assessees at risk. Not only might invalid selection decisions have been made, but the contracting organizations might have been held liable for these decisions.

The behavior of the psychologist's colleagues in this case must also be questioned. Knowing that a psychologist was practicing outside of his area of expertise and taking no action were ethically problematic. Informal consultation would have been appropriate to attempt to resolve the ethical concerns. If that failed, referral to an ethics committee or licensing board would then need to be considered.

D. Case Implications

Personnel selection issues are complicated and should be applied only by those individuals who are competent to do so. A psychologist who wishes to cross-train to develop new competencies may certainly do so. In the absence of a degree in I/O psychology, appropriate retraining might include formal course work, continuing education, study, consultation, and/or supervised experience. In the event that such training or consultation has not been obtained, the psychologist should refrain from offering services in those areas unless supervised by an appropriately trained professional. Psychological duties and responsibilities should always be reserved for demonstrated areas of competency and qualifications. Clinical or other psychologists applying their training to industrial applications should let it be known that their qualifications are in clinical psychology and not I/O psychology and appropriately limit the scope of their practice.

Of course a professional is not restricted forever to practicing in areas of graduate school training. It is certainly possible to cross-train or add specialties or competencies over the course of a career. Indeed, innovations in procedures, techniques, or knowledge often derive from such interdisciplinary applications. However, there is a clear difference between making such changes in a systematic and a haphazard way. In the case of innovative or emerging areas for which appropriate supervisors and/or knowledge are not yet available, psychologists in any specialty area need to proceed cautiously, with due regard for the limitations of knowledge or proficiency. In such instances, appropriate assistance might be obtained from persons with related, if not exactly identical, experience.

Additionally, psychologists who are aware of the potentially unethical behavior of another psychologist should normally approach the individual and discuss the competency concerns and the possible violations of the ethics code. Appropriate professional help, training, and/or supervision by

I/O professionals with experience in the areas and techniques needed by the organization could be suggested. If the psychologist is not responsive to informal consultations, the professional aware of the potential ethical violations then has an obligation to consider further action, including, if appropriate, reporting the violation to appropriate ethical or licensing bodies.

Case 47

Licensing and Credentialing

A. Statement of the Problem

An I/O psychologist started a consulting practice in a state requiring all psychologists, regardless of area of specialty, to be licensed prior to providing any psychological services to the public for a fee. The psychologist had been licensed in another state. The psychologist's practice involved the administration of standardized group tests and interviewing for the purpose of personnel screening. The practice excluded personality testing and health service activities.

Upon learning about her new state's licensure requirements, she contacted the licensing board. She was told that to be eligible to take the licensure examination, it was necessary to have worked under the supervision of a licensed psychologist for a period of 2 years after receipt of the doctoral degree. There was no reciprocity agreement between her present state and the one in which she had been licensed. The former state had a different licensing law, more compatible with the typical preparation of I/O psychologists. Since the psychologist previously had been employed by a state agency as a personnel psychologist reporting to the agency's personnel director (who was not a psychologist), it was not possible to meet her new state's requirements without additional preparation. The psychologist was therefore not permitted to take the licensing examination.

The psychologist decided to ignore the state requirement for licensure and to continue practicing, using the label of "Industrial/Organizational Psychologist," and to perform the tasks and duties which were psychological and which were controlled by law in the state. Her business cards and stationery identified her practice as being in "Industrial/Organizational Psychology." Her promotional materials described her as being a psychologist and listed several areas of practice with the word "psychology" in them.

The psychologist was contacted by a company exploring the possibility of her conducting some executive assessments. During one of the exploratory discussions, the organizational representative asked her if she was licensed as a psychologist. She stated that she was, without mentioning that her license was in another state. The company hired the psychologist for the work. Subsequently, in a forensic matter which arose concerning one of the assessments she performed for the company, the psychologist was disqualified as an expert witness for her client organization on the basis of her not being licensed to practice psychology in her state.

B. Ethics Code Standards

> **Ethical Standard 3.03   Avoidance of False or Deceptive Statements**
>
> **(a) Psychologists do not make public statements that are false, deceptive, misleading, or fraudulent, either because of what they state, convey, or suggest or because of what they omit, concerning their research, practice, or other work activities or those of persons or organizations with which they are affiliated. . . .**

C. Case Interpretation

In this case, the psychologist appears to have been in violation of a state law when, contrary to specific statute, she provided services that were required by that state only to be performed by a licensed psychologist. She made the situation worse by misleading a potential client as to the nature of her licensure. The client was potentially adversely affected subsequently when the reality of her situation became apparent.

The psychologist should have been familiar with the laws governing the practice of psychology before setting up her practice. The Ethics Code in its aspirational (nonenforceable) sections states that "[p]sychologists comply with the law . . ." (Principle F). The psychologist erred especially by not considering the requirements for licensure before she undertook independent practice. It was her professional responsibility to know the licensure laws in her state and to assure that she was in compliance, regardless of whether or not she personally agreed that licensure of I/O psychologists was a good or appropriate thing. Assuming she did not agree that I/O psychologists should be covered by the law, the code stipulates (in its enforceable provisions) that in situations in which there is a conflict between law and desirable practice, psychologists act responsibly to resolve the conflict. There appears to have been no attempt in this case to have changed the law or to address problems with its applicability to the I/O psychology specialty.

Because this psychologist was precluded by law from practicing psychology without holding a license, she should not have represented herself to organizations for which she proposed to work as practicing psychology or as being a psychologist. Of course, she could have made arrangements to work under the supervision of a licensed psychologist, or she might also have established her practice in a way that did not require violating the law. Alternatively, she could have limited her practice to areas not covered by the licensure act or worked with the licensure board to modify its licensure requirements so that I/O psychologists' needs were accommodated.

D. Case Implications

Psychologists are generally expected to comply with state licensure requirements when they include in their purview the practice and professional activities of I/O psychologists. There are a number of options available to I/O psychologists unable to meet the requirements for licensure in their states or who find the provisions of such laws to be inappropriate and unnecessary. They may arrange for any required supervision and then reapply for licensure at a later date. Alternatively, I/O psychologists might use titles other than "psychologist" (such as "personnel consultant") if the state's licensing law is a "title" rather than a "practice" law. Practice laws preclude the performance of defined activities except by those holding a license to do so.

Affected I/O psychologists should also consider working to change inappropriate licensure requirements. If state requirement for extensive postdoctoral supervision by a licensed psychologist prior to taking the licensing exam is unreasonable, psychologists can work with the state psychological association or licensing board and with other I/O psychologists in the state to revise the requirements. Of course an affected psychologist might also set up practice in a different state with alternative licensure requirements or those not requiring I/O psychologists to be licensed. Even if exempted from licensure laws, I/O psychologists have the ethical obligation to practice competently and within the restrictions of their areas of expertise.

Part VI

Billing and Marketing Issues

Case 48

Questions of Billing, Competence, and Supervision

A. Statement of the Problem

A consulting firm of I/O psychologists was hired by a large company to redesign its entire recruitment and selection system. A listing by name of specific individuals to perform each phase of the project (person-hours-by-task), along with specific hourly rates for each person to work on the project, was presented in the business section of the proposal.

Shortly before beginning the contracted work, one of the firm's senior-level I/O psychologists whose hours and rate had been itemized in the proposal and who was to have been a key staff member on the project left the firm to accept a position with another company. This psychologist was to have developed a particular assessment technique for inclusion in the selection system.

No one else in the firm who had a comparable level of experience with the technique to be used on this project was available to work on this contract. However, an intern had coincidentally recently been placed in another department of the consulting firm and happened to be completing his doctoral dissertation on the same technique. The project director, in consultation with other key managers in the firm, decided to transfer the intern to the group working on the new contract. Because of his experience and interest in this particular methodology, he was made an associate director of the project, a flattering role to the intern. The intern's hourly rate was substantially less than that of the psychologist who had left. The client was not advised of the specific nature of the change of staff.

The intern received very general direction from the project's director. The director had planned to try to arrange for the intern to consult occasionally with a more knowledgeable psychologist in the firm who was working on other projects at the time. Unfortunately, the director became preoccupied with other aspects of the project and with his other assignments. Because the project director observed that the intern seemed very confident, having never asked for technical assistance and having mentioned occasional consultations with the intern's academic advisor, he allowed him to work fairly independently.

In meetings with the client, it was never mentioned that a key part of the work was being done by an intern. The matter was regarded within the firm as being a relatively insignificant and fairly routine matter; staff come and staff go. Somehow it never seemed relevant to the discussion to review in detail the changes with representatives of the client organization.

The project was completed on schedule. Although the client was satisfied with all of the consulting work and the final products, the principals of the consulting firm privately felt that a better product could have been delivered. Without mentioning this to the intern, the firm's partners considered the intern's work to have been adequate but inferior to the firm's customary standards.

B. Ethics Code Standards

Ethical Standard 1.22   Delegation to and Supervision of Subordinates

(a) Psychologists delegate to their employees, supervisees, and research assistants only those responsibilities that such persons can reasonably be expected to perform competently, on the basis of their education, training, or experience, either independently or with the level of supervision being provided. (b) Psychologists provide proper training and supervision to their employees or supervisees and take reasonable steps to see that such persons perform services responsibly, competently, and ethically.

Ethical Standard 1.25   Fees and Financial Arrangements

(a) As early as is feasible ... the psychologist and the ... client ... reach an agreement specifying the compensation and the billing arrangements.
(b) Psychologists do not exploit recipients of services or payors with respect to fees.
(c) Psychologists' fee practices are consistent with law.
(d) Psychologists do not misrepresent their fees.

Ethical Standard 1.26   Accuracy in Reports to Payors and Funding Sources

In their reports to payors for services or sources of research funding, psychologists accurately state the nature of the research or service provided, the fees or charges, and where applicable, the identity of the provider....

Ethical Standard 6.05   Assessing Student and Supervisee Performance

(a) In academic and supervisory relationships, psychologists

establish an appropriate process for providing feedback to students and supervisees.

C. Case Interpretation

The fact that the client was satisfied with all of the deliverables is only one factor to be considered in evaluating the behavior described in this case. Several ethical concerns arise. First, the client was not informed of the originally designated psychologist's departure when it occurred or given an explicit promise that an equally qualified replacement would be made. If such a person were not available, the consulting firm could have offered, but did not, modification or cancellation of the contract.

The firm was also silent about the replacement being an intern and about the intern's compensation rate. The firm's principals apparently rationalized that the client was satisfied, the intern was not unqualified, and the difference between the actual and billed rates was small in proportion to the total contract price. Third, the project director was professionally remiss in not providing proper technical supervision, relying instead on alleged assistance from the intern's advisor. Fourth, the firm knowingly compromised the quality of its services.

D. Case Implications

When there are changes in a psychologist's or consulting firm's circumstances that potentially alter the terms of an agreement with a client or could compromise the quality of the services to be rendered, psychologists are ethically bound to tell the client about the changes and to offer a review of the original terms of the agreement. This obligation of honesty holds even when the circumstances of the changes are unavoidable and when they would not affect the outcome of the work.

As supervisors of persons-in-training, psychologists are obligated to trainees, clients with whom they work, and to trainees' home institutions to provide training experiences that are primarily for the benefit of the trainee. A psychologist or firm agreeing to provide such training has an obligation to assure that the learning experiences are valuable and adequately supervised. Training experiences undertaken simply to provide a cheap source of labor are potentially exploitative. Interns put into casually supervised settings, in addition to potentially being trained inadequately, may falsely assume that such conditions are professionally appropriate.

Case 49

Accurately and Honestly Marketing Psychological Products

A. Statement of the Problem

A faculty member of an I/O psychology program and two doctoral level graduate students developed a supervisory training program to be used as an exercise in an undergraduate class. The program was designed to demonstrate the application of behavior modification principles in industry and to illustrate how some problems business managers encounter can be helped by a knowledge of psychology.

One of the students in the course brought the training program to the attention of a relative, an economist by training, who was a successful management consultant. The relative approached the psychologist about the possibility of marketing the program. The psychologist decided he had nothing to lose by signing a contract giving the consultant exclusive rights to the program in exchange for a royalty payment. The psychologist would be allowed to continue using the program in classes and intended to do so. The psychologist felt that the program was not only a good teaching tool but also a way of researching issues associated with supervisory practices.

The psychologist planned to conduct research with students, to write an article or two based on this research, and to use the data to demonstrate the value of the program. The relative proceeded to market the program as "an effective tool for changing organizations," despite the fact that the instrument's effectiveness had never been evaluated.

B. Ethics Code Standards

Ethical Standard 1.16   Misuse of Psychologists' Work

(a) Psychologists do not participate in activities in which it appears likely that their skills or data will be misused by others, unless corrective mechanisms are available.
(b) If psychologists learn of misuse or misrepresentation of their work, they take reasonable steps to correct or minimize the misuse or misrepresentation.

Ethical Standard 1.19   Exploitative Relationships

(a) Psychologists do not exploit persons over whom they have supervisory, evaluative, or other authority such as students...[and] supervisees....

Ethical Standard 3.02   Statements by Others

(b) ... Psychologists make reasonable efforts to prevent others whom they do not control (such as employers, publishers, sponsors, organizational clients, and representatives of the print or broadcast media) from making deceptive statements concerning psychologists' practice or professional or scientific activities.
(c) If psychologists learn of deceptive statements about their work made by others, psychologists make reasonable efforts to correct such statements.

Ethical Standard 3.03   Avoidance of False or Deceptive Statements

(a) Psychologists do not make public statements that are false, deceptive, misleading, or fraudulent, either because of what they state, convey, or suggest or because of what they omit, concerning their research, practice, or other work activities or those of persons or organizations with which they are affiliated.

Ethical Standard 6.23   Publication Credit

(b) Principal authorship and other publication credits accurately reflect the relative scientific or professional contributions of the individuals involved, regardless of their relative status.

C. Case Interpretation

Many issues may be involved here. Some are obviously present; others may or may not arise depending on how the program was specifically developed and used. The case concerns the psychologist's professional responsibilities in developing adequate materials and in controlling how they are used, and the psychologist's obligations to students as colleagues.

Several ethical issues must be considered. First, there is the issue of whether a psychologist should sell a training program such as this one when it was devised as a classroom teaching tool and its effectiveness as a supervisory training aid is unknown. The psychologist also involved graduate students in the work without obtaining their consent, or having them share in the royalties from the program. Questions also must be considered about the psychologist's responsibility for how the program is used by others who sell and implement the program including the marketing claims made about the program's effectiveness. Relatedly, there is a potential problem raised by the program's generalizability beyond the classroom setting in which it was developed.

Psychologists should try to assure that a service or product developed and subsequently sold by someone other than themselves is used and marketed appropriately. Since the technique in this case was not formally or otherwise evaluated concerning its usefulness in training managers, claims for its effectiveness were limited. This should have been made clear to the consultant wishing to purchase the rights to the program prior to allowing it to be distributed.

The psychologist either should have evaluated the program's effectiveness himself or had the consultant arrange to do so, before releasing the instrument for publication. The psychologist should also have been careful to specify in the contract how the program was to be used and preferably that it would be marketed in accord with psychologists' ethical guidelines. Care should also have been taken to assure that the program was not misrepresented to prospective clients.

If the psychologist did conduct the needed evaluation research and used student populations to do so, the potential limitations and results (such as degree of generalizability to work settings) would need to be specified in any technical or commercially available reports. As the psychologist's research develops, any findings supporting or not supporting the program's effectiveness should also be communicated in the manuals or other documenting literature on the instrument.

Regarding the graduate students' potential claim to publication credit, or to financial or other rights in the program, the ethical issues depend on the specific contributions made and agreements reached. While the psychologist might argue that developing the program contributed to the students' professional development, publication credit may still be needed. Even if the faculty member legitimately claimed ownership of the idea for the program and primary responsibility for overseeing its development, publication credit would still be appropriate if the actual contributions of the students were substantial.

Concerning the graduate students' involvement in financial matters, the same general principles apply. Agreements regarding financial remuneration generally should be made in advance and should be consistent with the contribution made and the specific agreements reached. Various arrangements would have been possible, as appropriate, such as shared royalties paid in proportion to relative contribution or a onetime "buyout" payment. Above all, the issue should be clarified in advance of any work, or, as in this case, as soon as it becomes evident that the product is to be a commercial one. Since the project was developed under the auspices of the professor's employer, depending on its policies on such matters, the university might also have had a legitimate financial stake in the outcome.

D. Case Implications

Spin-offs of professional work are not per se an ethical concern. Special care is needed in such circumstances, however, because the many issues, financial and otherwise, created by commercial publications may not have been thought through.

Psychologists must always guard against misrepresentation of their products by themselves and others. This is especially important when a psychologist sells a product to a nonpsychologist who may not be bound by the same ethical principles. The psychologist's control may be diminished unless contractual agreements are made at the outset.

They must also take care to treat collaborators in a fair manner. Psychologists should recognize the contributions of graduate students just as they would recognize those of other colleagues. Above all, such agreements should be made early on in the working relationship. Additionally, the rights of other relevant parties, such as employers, to work developed as part of official duties need to be taken into account.

Case 50

Public Statements and Advertising

A. Statement of the Problem

An I/O psychology practitioner developed and began conducting a workshop for managers on selection testing. The goal of the seminar was primarily to attract managers to the seminars who would subsequently, it was hoped, become organizational consulting clients. A seminar promotions firm with a reputation for aggressive and successful marketing was contracted to promote and market the training program. In accordance with the firm's request, the psychologist provided a copy of a resume and a photograph for promotional purposes. The psychologist was sent copies of the materials used to market the product after they had been distributed. He did not raise any objections to the materials.

In time, the psychologist received a letter of inquiry from an ethics committee with relevant jurisdiction. A copy of the marketing materials was enclosed. The psychologist, who held a master's degree in I/O psychology, was described in the literature using the title "Dr.," and it was stated that he was "internationally renowned," even though his practice was limited to one state and he had never published anything in the professional literature. In the promotional materials, a list of attributes included the term "licensed psychologist," although the legally allowed terminology for someone licensed in his state at the master's level was "psychological assistant."

The brochure also described the psychologist's services and the promised results of the seminars in a manner which would appear to a layperson to be scientifically documented (e.g., "Permanently Stop Unwanted Turnover Without Increasing Your Labor Costs!"; "99% Effective!"). The brochure advised the potential purchaser that there were "Guaranteed Positive Results or Triple Your Money Back." In fact, an individual who had attended the seminar and found the seminars to be of limited use complained to the state licensing board after he had requested the triple refund and was turned down. Instead, he had been offered the chance to send an additional participant to a subsequent offering without charge.

In response to the ethics inquiry, the psychologist sent a letter from the president of the marketing firm stating that his firm, not the psychologist, was responsible for the promotional materials and that the offending items would be corrected, if possible, on the next marketing campaign. The psychologist noted that the guarantee was a business necessity in the competitive market in which he practiced. The respondent did note that financial exigencies made it impossible for him to reimburse the seminar tuition at triple the original payment but offered instead to permit the complaining party to send three rather than one participants to his next seminar at no charge. There were no empirical data to support the claims of effectiveness or the lack of impact on labor costs claimed in the brochure.

B. Ethics Code Standards

Ethical Standard 3.01   Definition of Public Statements

Psychologists comply with this Ethics Code in public statements relating to their professional services, products, or publications or to the field of psychology. Public statements include but are not limited to paid or unpaid advertising, brochures, printed matter, directory listings, personal resumes or curricula vitae, interviews or comments for use in media, statements in legal proceedings, lectures and public oral presentations, and published materials.

Ethical Standard 3.02   Statements by Others

(a) Psychologists who engage others to create or place public statements that promote their professional practice, products, or activities retain professional responsibility for such statements.
(c) If psychologists learn of deceptive statements about their work made by others, psychologists make reasonable efforts to correct such statements.

Ethical Standard 3.03   Avoidance of False or Deceptive Statements

(a) Psychologists do not make public statements that are false, deceptive, misleading, or fraudulent, either because of what they state, convey, or suggest or because of what they omit, concerning their research, practice, or other work activities or those of persons or organizations with which they are affiliated. As examples (and not in limitation) of this standard, psychologists do not make false or deceptive statements concerning (1) their training, experience, or competence; (2) their academic degrees; (3) their credentials; (4) their institutional or association affiliations; (5) their services; (6) the scientific or clinical basis for, or results or de-

gree of success of, their services; (7) their fees; or (8) their publications or research findings.

C. Case Interpretation

This case concerns the responsibility of a psychologist when making (or contracting to have made) public statements, announcements of services, advertising, or promotional activities. In this case, the information in the brochure was factually incorrect and misleading. The psychologist ethically retains the responsibility for accuracy even when contracting with a firm to do the marketing or promotional work. It is the obligation and responsibility of a professional psychologist to examine promotional materials and to request the right of prior approval before distribution to the general public. This is particularly true when the psychologist has not had prior experience with a marketer's promotional practices and when a marketer has not previously marketed psychological services or is otherwise insensitive to the demands for honesty and accuracy in professional marketing efforts. If proposed marketing materials are incompatible with ethical standards, the psychologist should insist on correction prior to distribution. At the least, the psychologist should have taken corrective action as soon as he received the marketing materials.

Another ethical concern in this case occurred in the promised results and the guarantee of benefit. The outcome claims made by the brochure (e.g., to permanently end turnover) were unsubstantiated and likely to be false, deceptive, or misleading. Although it could be argued that the "triple guarantee" was sensationalistic, the Ethics Code does not regulate the manner of advertising, as long as the content is not false, misleading, or deceptive. If a psychologist makes a money-back guarantee, he or she has the obligation to honor it, which in this case did not happen.

D. Case Implications

This case highlights an issue faced by many consulting I/O psychologists. Services must be sold in an increasingly competitive business environment. Marketing techniques that are possibly common in business may well include guarantees or "puffery." Even in competitive markets, psychologists must still adhere to the ethical standards regarding public statements which are designed to protect the basic rights to accuracy of those whom they serve and to avoid false or deceptive statements to potential clients.

Psychologists who participate in programs in which publicity and other marketing efforts will be executed by others must make reasonable efforts to anticipate the possibility of misrepresentation or misleading potential clients or customers. It remains the psychologist's responsibility, regardless of whether or not direct control of marketing was obtained, to assure that public statements made by or on behalf of a psychologist are consistent with relevant ethical guidelines. By insisting on a contract or agreement which gives the psychologist the right to review promotional materials, there is less likelihood of misleading advertising or deception. When ethically problematic promotional efforts for their practice come to their attention, psychologists are obligated to initiate efforts to change the ethically questionable practices.

Case 51 _____

Making Public Statements

A. Statement of the Problem

An employer settled a complex employment discrimination lawsuit by agreeing to hire an outside consulting firm that would be responsible for overseeing the development and validation of a new selection procedure intended to increase the company's numbers of protected class employees. The consulting firm was responsible for working closely with the employer's in-house psychologists to ensure that the new selection system was consistent with legal and professional standards. Although the in-house psychologists and the consulting firm's representatives agreed on the overall approach, the two groups disagreed on several specific issues. Resolving these differences required rather complicated and somewhat protracted negotiations between the two parties; both groups were forced to make some compromises. The consulting firm's psychologists were never very happy with the compromises and harbored resentment against the company's psychologists. They suggested to the company's management at one point that the company might want to consider replacing those psychologists, an action the company declined to take.

A few months after the project was completed, several psychologists from the consulting firm presented information from the project at a symposium held at a professional conference. The consulting firm did not invite any of the in-house psychologists or any neutral psychologists to participate and had not obtained permission from the client organization to present on the case. The consulting psychologists did not mention the in-house psychologists by name, but enough information about the project was identified that, since it was fairly visible within the profession, the psychologists whose stance was criticized were readily identifiable, as was their employer.

The psychologists from the consulting firm misrepresented, and then criticized, the work of the in-house psychologists. In their presentations, the consultants falsely implied that the in-house psychologists had been entirely responsible for the company's battles with the regulatory agency. They omitted significant factual information from their presentation that was essential for understanding the position the company's psychologists had taken. For example, they failed to mention that the in-house psychologists had aggressively fought within the company to stop the use of an unvalidated personnel selection instrument that had adverse impact. Instead the consultants implied incompetence on the part of the company's psychologists for allowing the use of the problematic instrument which had brought the company to the attention of the regulators. The consultants also took full credit for "rescuing" the company from the regulatory authorities, entirely inconsistent with the facts of the case.

The in-house psychologists, who were not present at the presentation but heard about it soon thereafter, obtained an audiotape of the presentation and complained to the consulting firm that the psychologists' presentation had misrepresented their views and the facts of the case. They insisted that the consultants stop the distribution of the audiotape and complained to the consulting firm's psychologists that they had, seemingly intentionally, misrepresented the facts of the case and had inappropriately identified their organizational client in a public forum.

B. Ethics Code Standards

Ethical Standard 1.15   Misuse of Psychologists' Influence

Because psychologists' scientific and professional judgments and actions may affect the lives of others, they are alert to and guard against personal, financial, social, organizational, or political factors that might lead to misuse of their influence.

Ethical Standard 3.03   Avoidance of False or Deceptive Statements

(a) Psychologists do not make public statements that are false, deceptive, misleading, or fraudulent, either because of what they state, convey, or suggest or because of what they omit, concerning their research, practice, or other work activities or those of persons or organizations with which they are affiliated....

Ethical Standard 5.08   Use of Confidential Information for Didactic or Other Purposes

(a) Psychologists do not disclose in their writings, lectures, or other public media, confidential, personally identifiable information concerning their ... organizational clients, ... unless the ... organization has consented in writing or unless there is other ethical or legal authorization for doing so.

(b) Ordinarily, in such scientific and professional presentations, psychologists disguise confidential information concerning such persons or organizations so that they are not individually identifiable to others and so that discussions do not cause harm to subjects who might identify themselves.

C. Case Interpretation

A number of ethical concerns arise from this case. First, the consulting firm's psychologists appeared to have violated their organizational client's confidentiality by making a public presentation on their work without that client's permission. The consulting psychologists neglected adequately to disguise the specific nature of the project so that members of the audience would not know the identity of the in-house psychologists or the identity of the company itself. The consulting firm's psychologists should also have obtained permission from their client organization to discuss the case at all in a public forum.

Second, the psychologists caused potential harm to their colleagues in the client organization by the manner of presentation. The consulting psychologists misrepresented the actions of their colleagues. They only presented one side of the arguments in a way that resulted in false and misleading statements being made about the project or the in-house psychologists' actions or motives.

Although it is not always essential to present opposing perspectives on an issue, misrepresentation by intentional distortion or exclusion is another matter entirely. It is certainly acceptable for psychologists openly to disagree with their colleagues, but if the views of those being criticized are not generally known or readily available, these individuals should be given the opportunity to respond or the intended audience members should at least be provided sufficient factual information that they could draw their own conclusions.

Finally, it appears that the consulting firm's psychologists were more intent on settling a score with their colleagues than on fairness and objectivity. The consultants' unhappiness with some of the conclusions reached in the various compromises that had to be made should not have been the basis for distortion of the facts of a case or other interpretations of the facts of a case at a scientific meeting. Nor should the public presentation have been used as the opportunity for retaliation or vindication.

D. Case Implications

When psychologists are involved in disagreements or adversarial relationships they should be particularly conscious of ethical concerns and parameters. This is especially true when making public statements about the work of other professionals who may hold opposing perspectives. It can certainly be tempting to use a presentation to satisfy a personal agenda or to curry support for a particular point of view. However, the ethical duty remains for psychologists to be objective and to be genuinely respectful of alternative points of view when commenting on other professionals and their work. To the extent they have reason to be aware of such matters, program planning committees should be alert to potential ethical conflicts in conference programs and should strive to assure that controversial programs will be balanced.

Part VII

The Ethics of
Professional Behavior

Case 52

Responding to Allegations of Misconduct

A. Statement of the Problem

A consulting psychologist was asked by an organizational client to facilitate a series of employee meetings on ways to improve departmental productivity. Following one of the employee meetings, the chief financial officer's (CFO) secretary privately approached the psychologist and indicated that she was certain that the CFO was embezzling company funds. The conversation lasted only a few minutes. The psychologist listened attentively and then indicated that she would notify company officials. She promised to keep confidential the secretary's identity.

After returning to her office, the psychologist described this conversation in a letter she sent to the company's Vice President of Human Resources, her contact at the client organization. In doing so, the psychologist honored her commitment to confidentiality. She also offered to assist the situation in any way possible, including the possibility of participating in a meeting with appropriate officials of the client organization. The Vice President of Human Resources accepted her offer and invited her to a meeting with a half dozen senior executives and the company's general counsel. Based on the allegations relayed by the psychologist, the executives agreed to conduct a full investigation.

The investigation was quite thorough and costly for the organization. It did not reveal any evidence of embezzlement or other financial wrongdoing. After a few months it became apparent that the secretary was actively engaged in a campaign to discredit the CFO.

B. Ethics Code Standards

Ethical Standard 1.14   Avoiding Harm

Psychologists take reasonable steps to avoid harming their patients or clients, research participants, students, and others with whom they work, and to minimize harm where it is foreseeable and unavoidable.

Ethical Standard 1.16   Misuse of Psychologists' Work

(a) Psychologists do not participate in activities in which it appears likely that their skills or data will be misused by others, unless corrective mechanisms are available. (See also Standard 7.04, Truthfulness and Candor.)
(b) If psychologists learn of misuse or misrepresentation of their work, they take reasonable steps to correct or minimize the misuse or misrepresentation.

C. Case Interpretation

The psychologist did not necessarily behave unethically in this case. She had listened carefully to the secretary's information, forwarded the charges to the appropriate organizational official, maintained confidentiality of the source of the allegation throughout the process, and offered to provide follow-up assistance (though if the psychologist were paid for this involvement, the possibility of conflicts of interest would need to be considered).

Still, there were other, perhaps more effective, approaches the psychologist might have taken, possibly with less potentially negative impact on a person who, in this instance, turned out to have been falsely accused. Instead of being the person to report the alleged wrongdoing, the psychologist might have explored ways in which the complaining party could have made the report herself. As a key employee in the financial department, the secretary presumably had her own obligations and responsibilities if she suspected or encountered financially inappropriate behavior. The psychologist might have explored with the employee ways to identify the company's procedures available for reporting, anonymously or otherwise, such behavior.

For her part, the psychologist might also have explored in a general way available options with the HR department. She then could have provided the information to the employee without personally becoming a key player in the matter. She might have arranged a meeting with company officials in which the allegations could have been aired to responsible parties in the organization.

D. Case Implications

Mixed or even malevolent motives are unfortunately not unknown when there are allegations of improper behavior by fellow employees or supervisors. Consulting psychologists may find themselves in positions in which they are exposed to this type of information (or misinformation). Employees may view the psychologist as being a convenient vehicle by which to express their concerns or allegations without suffering adverse consequences that might be associated with a more direct confrontation. The psychologist's role in such instances may be a legitimate one, helping to gather and assemble the perceptions of various employees and managers in determining whether there is a need for a more formal investigation. Alternatively, psychologists may unwittingly become messengers used to convey counterproductive or false information. Psychologists must always be sensitive to this possibility, especially in high-stakes situations. Although there may be a need to make decisions or take actions on the basis of incomplete data, psychologists should make every reasonable effort to ensure that the information they are acting on has been provided in good faith, that they are the most appropriate persons to initiate action, and that they do not themselves have potential conflicts of interest, including financial incentives.

Case 53 _____

The Ethics of Voluntary Professional Activities

A. Statement of the Problem

An I/O psychologist volunteered to be part of a task force for a large and prestigious national professional association. The work was somewhat tangential to the psychologist's day-to-day duties but represented an area of general interest to him, and he wanted to be involved with some of the widely recognized psychologists who were involved with the work. He felt that the involvement would be a valued part of his work activities by enhancing his prestige, knowledge, and professional colleagues. The psychologist's employer agreed to his participation, noting that it was desirable for the firm's staff to be professionally active and visible. The supervisor agreed that the professional association's activities could be done during work hours so long as his work activities did not suffer.

At the time of agreeing to serve on the task force, the psychologist knew that he was overextended at work. He further knew that he was in the midst of a difficult personal problem, a contested divorce, and that his attention would be diverted by these factors, according to his lawyers, for several years. He also was aware of his own track record in accepting such assignments in the past and not delivering what he had agreed to do.

Each participant on the task force was assigned by the Chair of the committee certain responsibilities, which included the collection of some survey research data. The goal was to create a position paper on an important topic with far-reaching implications for the practice of I/O psychology. When the deadline for the assignments to be returned came and went with none of the promised work having been submitted by the psychologist, the Chair of the task force called the individual several times to ask for an update. The calls were not returned. Because the project was to be completed on a very small budget, the costs of these calls had to be borne by the Chair.

Finally reached by the Chair, the psychologist ventilated a lengthy diatribe accusing the Chair of being unfair and unreasonable and noting his many personal commitments. A few weeks later, the psychologist sent a short written note to the Chair indicating, without explanation, that he was resigning from the task force. He never submitted his promised work and made no arrangements to have someone else complete it. The Chair had to do much of the work herself and to arrange a replacement on the Committee for the psychologist who resigned.

B. Ethics Code Standards

Ethical Standard 1.01   Applicability of the Ethics Code

The activity of a psychologist subject to the Ethics Code may be reviewed under these Ethical Standards ... if the activity is part of his or her work-related functions or the activity is psychological in nature.

Ethical Standard 1.13   Personal Problems and Conflicts

(a) Psychologists recognize that their personal problems and conflicts may interfere with their effectiveness. Accordingly, they refrain from undertaking an activity when they know or should know that their personal problems are likely to lead to harm to a patient, client, colleague, student, research participant, or other person to whom they may owe a professional or scientific obligation.

C. Case Interpretation

The psychologist's behavior was problematic in several ways. First, in making a commitment to work on a project, whether involving paid activities or not, the psychologist had an obligation not to allow personal problems to interfere with professional obligations. Not performing the agreed-upon activities caused harm to the project and to those with whom the psychologist had agreed to work.

Second, when it became clear that he could not fulfill his responsibilities to the project, it was his obligation to take appropriate action. Instead of initiating such action, he avoided the Committee's Chair and treated her angrily when she finally made contact with him. Several options might have been possible to the psychologist had he been proactive about his difficulties, including a revised deadline, assignment of some of the tasks to others on the Committee, or the psychologist's arranging for an acceptable replacement.

The psychologist's behavior caused financial harm to the Chair and to the project and further delayed the work's being done. His personal problems of overcommitment and emotional strain appeared to have contributed to his problematic behavior. It was not inappropriate for the psychologist to submit his resignation but not to have undertaken the assignment in the first place, or promptly taking action to prevent harm to others when the personal conflicts became apparent, would have been a superior course of action.

D. Case Implications

It is argued that psychologists' ethical obligations extend to all their work activities, whether performed for money or not. Personal motives such as desire for power or prestige more than professional service may drive decisions to contribute one's time to a voluntary work activity. When personal problems or conflicts interfere with the successful performance of these duties, ethical concerns arise.

It is understandable that at times obligations from paid employment may have to take precedence over volunteer activities. In such cases, the psychologist's ethical responsibility is to contact the manager of the project and negotiate an extension of time or arrange to be replaced for the duties previously agreed to be done. When, as a last resort, the psychologist must renege on prior commitments, he or she must take the initiative to minimize harm to the project and to colleagues. Appropriate actions may include arranging for a colleague to do the work or assisting the project's manager in finding a suitable replacement.

Case 54 _____

Professional and Scientific Responsibility in Forensic Activities

A. Statement of the Problem

Two psychologists were hired as expert witnesses by opposing sides in a state court case. The court ordered all witnesses, including experts, to be sequestered during the trial so that no witness would hear any other testimony prior to testifying. Both psychologists were informed of the court's order on the first day of trial. During the first psychologist's testimony, new and unexpected information was presented. The attorney for the other side wanted to be sure that this new information was addressed in the case.

On the same evening that the first psychologist had testified, the second psychologist met with his attorney to prepare for his testimony which was scheduled for the following day. During this meeting the attorney described how a "typical" opposing expert might testify, in the process revealing in detail the new information. Although the attorney did not indicate this was how the first expert had actually testified, the psychologist suspected this was the case. He did not pursue the issue. The psychologist did not change the specific content or major points of his testimony, but he was able to emphasize particular factors in his testimony which happened to address weaknesses in the other side's unexpected information.

B. Ethics Code Standards

Ethical Standard 7.06   Compliance With Law and Rules

In performing forensic roles, psychologists are reasonably familiar with the rules governing their roles. Psychologists are aware of the occasionally competing demands placed upon them by these principles and the requirements of the court system, and attempt to resolve these conflicts by making known their commitment to this Ethics Code and taking steps to resolve the conflict in a responsible manner.

C. Case Interpretation

The "coached" psychologist had an obligation to honor, in spirit as well as letter, the rules established by the Court especially the requirement that the expert witnesses not hear each other's testimony during the trial. Since the court had specifically mandated sequestered witnesses, it was not appropriate for the second psychologist to hear anything about the other side's testimony, whether this occurred directly or indirectly. The psychologist should have immediately clarified during the meeting with the attorney his commitment to honoring the court's order. Under the circumstances of the judge's order, it was inappropriate for him to have listened to, and failed to challenge, the attorney's coaching when there arose reasonable cause to suspect that the attorney was describing the first psychologist's testimony.

D. Case Implications

Psychologists who engage in forensic consultations or testimony should be aware of the similarities and differences between attorneys' and psychologists' obligations. Both professions are expected to abide by law and the court's rules. Attorneys, however, are generally hired to be advocates while psychologists must retain scientific neutrality and objectivity. Care must be taken by psychologists offering court testimony that they do not allow the adversarial circumstances of a trial to compromise their objectivity or obligations to comply with the law.

Case 55 _____

A Change of Career Direction

A. *Statement of the Problem*

After completing graduate training in I/O psychology with a special emphasis on performance measurement, an I/O psychologist worked for several years in the HR research and development function of a large organization. The group, headed by an I/O psychologist, conducted job analyses, designed selection and performance appraisal systems, and conducted attitude surveys.

When the clinical psychologist responsible for the organization's EAP unexpectedly quit, the I/O psychologist working in the HR Department volunteered to manage the function until a replacement could be found. The position involved supervising a small support staff, instituting and monitoring referral systems, and assessing and counseling employees. Although she had no applied clinical experience or supervised training, the I/O psychologist had taken several clinical psychology courses in graduate school and had a long-standing interest in the clinical side of applied psychology. In addition, she had extensive knowledge of the organization and familiarity with the problems of many of the employees. The I/O psychologist felt that this background would be sufficient for her to manage the function. Additionally, she had always wanted to learn more about counseling.

After a month on the job, the I/O psychologist decided to apply for the position herself. Not only was the job interesting, but it also offered an opportunity to learn an area of applied psychology new to her. It also would provide her management experience which was not presently a possibility in the research and development function.

In applying for the position, the I/O psychologist revised her resume, emphasizing her PhD in psychology, rather than her specialization in I/O psychology, and stressing her clinical course work. She asked for the support of her somewhat skeptical manager. Although her boss was concerned about the psychologist's appropriateness for the clinical aspects of the job, she convinced him that the EAP position primarily required managerial skills and that she was well suited for such a role.

Because of her experience with the organization and the positive recommendation of her manager, the I/O psychologist was selected for this position and began her "on-the-job training" to learn the clinical and managerial responsibilities of the EAP manager's position.

B. Ethics Code Standards

Ethical Standard 1.04   Boundaries of Competence

(a) Psychologists provide services ... only within the boundaries of their competence, based on their education, training, supervised experience, or appropriate professional experience.
(b) Psychologists provide services, teach, or conduct research in new areas or involving new techniques only after first undertaking appropriate study, training, supervision, and/or consultation from persons who are competent in those areas or techniques.

Ethical Standard 3.03   Avoidance of False or Deceptive Statements

(a) Psychologists do not make public statements that are false, deceptive, misleading, or fraudulent, either because of what they state, convey, or suggest or because of what they omit, concerning their research, practice, or other work activities.... [P]sychologists do not make false or deceptive statements concerning (1) their training, experience, or competence; (2) their academic degrees; [or] (3) their credentials....

Ethical Standard 8.02   Confronting Ethical Issues

When a psychologist is uncertain whether a particular situation or course of action would violate this Ethics Code, the psychologist ordinarily consults with other psychologists knowledgeable about ethical issues, with state or national psychology ethics committees, or with other appropriate authorities in order to choose a proper response.

C. Case Interpretation

The I/O psychologist in this case appears to have attempted to change career directions without benefit of appropriate preparation. It was not necessarily ethically problematic for a psychologist to seek or assume responsibility for managing an EAP program since, to some extent, managerial skills are generic. In this case, however, a psychologist with no clinical/counseling psychological training and apparently with no managerial experience or training actively sought a move in which both skill sets were relevant.

A particular problem arose because the EAP manager was also called upon to manage clinical casework and had only had minimal, and introductory, course work in this area. Learning-by-doing, while not uncommon in specific industrial applications of psychology, is not an appropriate way to learn counseling or psychotherapy.

Not only was the new EAP manager's behavior ethically questionable but so was that of her superior. The organization's decision makers were possibly unaware of the ethical obligations of psychologists and of the educational and training requirements for specific applied positions. They reasonably would rely on the expertise of their in-house psychologists in such matters. The managing psychologist should have insisted that the position be filled by someone with appropriate training and background. If his subordinate's fitness for this particular position was in question, he could have obtained information from other psychologists and from managers of EAP programs in other companies rather than relying solely on the psychologist's persuasive abilities as a basis for action.

D. Case Implications

Fine lines sometimes arise in applied settings between what a psychologist is prepared to do and what, with reasonable preparation, a psychologist can become competent to do. It is not unethical or unreasonable for a psychologist to learn by on-the-job experience a new technique or application. Appropriate learning activities, including supervision, are necessary when the technique requires knowledge or methods that cannot be obtained through self-learning alone.

Psychologists have an ethical obligation always to recognize the boundaries of their competencies and not to attempt a major shift of direction without appropriate training. This is true no matter what economic pressures for diversification may apply in specific areas of practice.

Because applied industrial settings often look more to judged ability than to credentials or training, those practicing psychology within organizations should be especially aware of the limits of their training and the boundaries of their specialty. Switching from one applied psychological specialty to another requires appropriate learning experiences and supervision to serve the needs of clients and to meet professional standards.

Case 56

Plagiarizing

A. Statement of the Problem

An I/O psychology graduate student wrote a dissertation in a specialized area relating to personnel selection. Only one of the faculty members in his program had detailed knowledge of the specific area, and he had died in the last stages of the student's dissertation work. This faculty member had been the graduate student's major thesis advisor. Under the circumstances, another professor agreed to serve as the student's dissertation chair, even though this was not her area of specialization.

The dissertation included several sections, using identical wording, from a colleague's dissertation completed several years earlier. The work of the colleague was never cited, and the colleague was never mentioned in the body of the dissertation or even noted in the reference list. The student successfully defended his dissertation and earned his doctorate.

After graduating, the I/O psychologist published a portion of the dissertation, including an introduction which was substantially similar to the colleague's earlier work. Again, no credit was given to the original author of the material. The original author, who had maintained an interest in the topic of his dissertation, happened to read one of the articles in which his work had been used. He contacted the author, who insisted that he had no knowledge of the work being overlapping.

Dissatisfied with the cavalier manner in which he perceived his protest was handled by the university's psychology department when the issue was brought to its attention, the original author wrote to the editor of the relevant journal and to the university that granted the student's degree and reported the finding. He asked both groups to take appropriate action, and each opened an investigation, which, for the university, included as a possible outcome, the revocation of the doctoral degree. He also filed an ethics complaint with a professional association to which the psychologist belonged and with the state licensing board that had granted the psychologist a license. The respondent refused to cooperate with the professional association's ethics panel, noting that he was a student at the time of the alleged infraction and that the ethics standards were therefore not enforceable for behavior said to occur at that time.

B. Ethics Code Standards

Ethical Standard 6.22   Plagiarism

Psychologists do not present substantial portions or elements of another's work or data as their own, even if the other work or data source is cited occasionally.

Ethical Standard 6.23   Publication Credit

(b) Principal authorship and other publication credits accurately reflect the relative scientific or professional contributions of the individuals involved, regardless of their relative status. . . .

Ethical Standard 8.05   Reporting Ethical Violations

If an apparent ethical violation is not appropriate for informal resolution under Standard 8.04 or is not resolved properly in that fashion, psychologists take further action. . . . Such action might include referral to state or national committees on professional ethics or to state licensing boards.

Ethical Standard 8.06   Cooperating With Ethics Committees

Psychologists cooperate in ethics investigations, proceedings, and resulting requirements of the APA or any affiliated state psychological association to which they belong. . . .

C. Case Interpretation

This case involves two potential issues, one more complex than the violation of ethical standards reflected in the plagiarism. Clearly it is unethical for a psychologist to use materials involving the exact wording from another person's dissertation without the consent of the original writer and without the appropriate citation. To have published the work of another professional involves violations of ethical standards as well as of copyright laws if the earlier work had been copyrighted.

The other difficult issue in this case concerns the individual's status as a student of psychology at the time of the problematic behavior. Although the Ethical Principles of Psychologists have applicability to students of psychology as well as to practicing psychologists, the ethics may not be enforceable against students unless they are members of associations (or persons licensed by boards) endorsing the codes. Responsibility for addressing allegations of unethical behavior of graduate students rests primarily with the psychology faculty members most directly responsible for the students' education. If the faculty members supervising the dissertation research in this case were aware of the plagiarism, they should certainly have confronted the issue and taken appropriate action in accordance with the rules of their university and academic department in which the behavior occurred.

Since the now-deceased major professor was the one most intimately familiar with this specific area of research, the supervising faculty may have been unaware of the unethical behavior. Action still should have been taken to confront the issue once it was brought to the department's attention. Some universities, for example, have revoked doctoral degrees when evidence of plagiarism has been discovered after conferring degrees.

Appropriate action by the university is particularly important since educational institutions have a special responsibility for modeling the principles and behavior which they are training. Failure to confront unethical behavior by students in training can set a bad example. Finally, if the violation were discovered, as in this case, by the psychologist whose dissertation was copied, or by others who knew the material was plagiarized, these parties would have an obligation to address the unethical behavior.

D. Case Implications

There is no excuse for plagiarism in psychological research, particularly when it is possible to make use of other's work so long as appropriate attribution is made and appropriate permissions obtained. When plagiarism is discovered, it should be dealt with vigorously, since honesty and integrity are important elements of the research process.

Psychology departments need to have operating rules for dealing with complaints of unethical behavior on the part of students. Graduate committees should also be sensitive to the possibility of ethical violations by their students and, most importantly, be prepared to act when cases come to their attention. Only by doing so can psychologists contribute to the maintenance of the acceptable ethical practice.

Case 57 _____

Evaluating Colleagues' Competencies

A. Statement of the Problem

An I/O psychologist who conducted individual executive assessments for a long-term client was asked by a key manager in the organization for an opinion of the work of a second psychologist who was being considered for a personnel selection contract with the organization. This was a somewhat sensitive project which might entail forensic work.

The first psychologist initially praised the reputation of the other psychologist, who was highly regarded professionally and well published in his area of expertise, but then proceeded to give examples of the psychologist's working style that were phrased in such a way as to subtly raise doubts about the psychologist's appropriateness for the assignment in question. In the conversation, the first psychologist, who had little forensic background or experience and whose business had been affected by a recession in his geographic area, mentioned in passing that his firm had recently begun doing work in the personnel selection area in which the services were needed.

The company opted not to pursue the relationship with the psychologist whose work was commented upon and made no further contact with that psychologist. The manager instead contracted for the consulting services of the psychologist with whom the organization had an ongoing relationship. The work was accomplished at a satisfactory level, and the psychologist was able to expand his practice in new directions.

B. Ethics Code Standards

Ethical Standard 1.06   Basis for Scientific and Professional Judgments

Psychologists rely on scientifically and professionally derived knowledge when making scientific or professional judgments or when engaging in scholarly or professional endeavors.

Ethical Standard 1.17   Multiple Relationships

(a) ... A psychologist refrains from entering into or promising

another personal, scientific, professional, financial, or other relationship with such persons if it appears likely that such a relationship reasonably might impair the psychologist's objectivity or otherwise interfere with the psychologist's effectively performing his or her function as a psychologist, or might harm or exploit the other party.

C. Case Interpretation

This case primarily concerns a psychologist's professional relationships with other psychologists and the well-being of the consumers of psychological services. Had he not subsequently suggested himself for the services in question, the psychologist who had the long-standing relationship with the organization may or may not have behaved inappropriately in evaluating his colleague. The appropriateness of the behavior would in such circumstances depend on the specific evaluation that was intended to be communicated and the psychologist's motivation.

The psychologist had a professional obligation to provide a professional evaluation to the manager in the client organization requesting it. At the same time he was obliged to evaluate the second psychologist in a manner that avoided damage to his/her professional reputation or otherwise causing harm. If the first psychologist had legitimate reservations about the second psychologist's appropriateness for this assignment, that information was appropriate to communicate, providing the reasons and evidence in support of that in such a manner that the manager could objectively formulate his own opinion. The same should have been done if the offered opinions of the second psychologist were favorable. Because evaluating another's professional reputation is often difficult and may fall outside a psychologist's specific competency, the person requesting the opinion might be referred to other professionals (or, if known, to client organizations) for additional opinions.

Once the psychologist attempted to bid for the business himself, the situation became especially problematic. When, as in this case, a psychologist assumes roles of evaluating the competition and marketing services for one's own group, it potentially constitutes a dual (or multiple) relationship, and should be avoided. Objectivity suffers in such circumstances, and the psychologist should have removed himself from making the evaluation. Alternatively, the first psychologist could have rendered his opinion and recognized that it was then ethically inappropriate for him to attempt to gain the business for himself.

Finally, there is the question of the evaluating psychologist's own competence for doing the work in question. Since he was not experienced in the specific area of the work, which had potential forensic aspects, his appropriateness for the assignment is not clear.

D. Case Implications

It is not unethical to evaluate for a client or employer the competence, style, or approach of another psychologist, even when that evaluation is negative. When such evaluations are governed by self-interest, they become ethically questionable. Psychologists need to determine before making such evaluations whether they can be objective in making and communicating the assessment. The limitations of the psychologist's objectivity need to be made clear. Psychologists also need to recognize that subtle comments may be taken to mean negative ones and refrain from damning colleagues' work by implication or innuendo. If there are problems or concerns, these need to be stated frankly, providing the basis for the opinions and conclusion, and suggesting alternative ways in which the opinion can be verified or challenged.

Psychologists need to understand that their views about the professional competencies of a colleague are often the primary basis on which a decision may be made by a prospective client. Psychologists asked to provide their opinions on the worth or appropriateness of their colleagues' work must do so with integrity and not in a way primarily intended to further their own gain. If a psychologist has any misgivings about his or her ability to evaluate a colleague objectively, it may be more appropriate not to evaluate at all rather than to provide an opinion that may be misleading.

Case 58 _____

Confronting Unethical Behavior

A. Statement of the Problem

Two I/O psychologists, working as a team, claimed that they had achieved validity coefficients in the .90s for a sales representative inventory validated against criteria of sales success. Their data were published in a well-known business journal. A scatter diagram, substantiating this high correlation, was included in the published article. No explanation was provided for the unusual results. There was nothing particularly unusual about the sample items in the paper-and-pencil selection inventory, nor were the criterion measures unusual so there was reason to suspect the veracity of the reported results.

Several other reports examining the relationships between similar items and similar criteria had appeared in the published literature. Typically, the relationships found were substantially lower than those found in the business journal article. Since there was such clear agreement in the bulk of the reported research, it seemed likely that the data published in the article were faked or miscalculated. However, on the strength of that one report, the two I/O psychologists had been selling their test and services to numerous organizations for several years.

When queried about the article after its publication, the journal's editor, who was not a psychologist, remembered it well. The editor stated that something seemed not quite right about the claims made in the article but that no real grounds or real evidence was available to refuse to publish it. It was not the practice of this business journal at that time to use outside professionals as reviewers. The editor added that if anyone in the profession wanted to prepare a relevant review of the literature or to report more recent data showing correlations between similar variables, or between the same sales representative inventory and similar criteria, he, as the editor of the journal, would be glad to publish the material, making direct reference to the article containing the unusually high validity results. Several I/O psychologists discussed the matter and believed that the data must have been intentionally misrepresented. However, all were too busy to prepare a follow-up article, so nothing was ever done to challenge the original report.

B. Ethics Code Standards

Ethical Standard 6.25   Sharing Data

After research results are published, psychologists do not withhold the data on which their conclusions are based from other competent professionals who seek to verify the substantive claims through reanalysis and who intend to use such data only for that purpose, provided that the confidentiality of the participants can be protected and unless legal rights concerning proprietary data preclude their release.

Ethical Standard 8.04   Informal Resolution of Ethical Violations

When psychologists believe that there may have been an ethical violation by another psychologist, they attempt to resolve the issue by bringing it to the attention of that individual if an informal resolution appears appropriate....

Ethical Standard 8.05   Reporting Ethical Violations

If an apparent ethical violation is not appropriate for informal resolution under Standard 8.04 or is not resolved properly in that fashion, psychologists take further action appropriate to the situation, unless such action conflicts with confidentiality rights in ways that cannot be resolved. Such action might include referral to state or national committees on professional ethics or to state licensing boards.

C. Case Interpretation

This case involves a possible ethical violation in the published literature. Falsification or misrepresentation of data would constitute an ethics violation. There was reasonable cause to suspect the reported data because correlations of this magnitude are almost never found in the literature and the authors had a proprietary interest in the study's results. Several I/O psychologists believed there was misrepresentation at the least.

Even though the journal in question was not a psychological journal, psychologists were involved both in writing the article and in questioning its veracity. That the psychologists approached the journal editor with their concern suggests that they were aware of a possible ethics violation. While the psychologists doubting the findings might well not have had the time to write a review article for the business journal, they could certainly have raised their concerns with the psychologist–authors (composing a letter is seldom time-consuming) or have referred the matter to an ethics review board if the psychologist–authors proved unresponsive to such inquiries.

The psychologists with the concerns might have attempted to investigate their suspicions informally with the authors of the article as a first course of action. Suspecting falsified or otherwise manipulated data, and following Standard 6.25, they might have asked these authors for the data and reanalyzed it. They might also have asked the authors to clarify their findings or for an explanation of how these data might be so discrepant with the rest of the literature. If these informal methods did not lead to a resolution, the psychologists could have referred their complaint formally to an appropriate ethics committee for investigation.

Alternatively, if the psychologists feared that, were the authors tipped off about a possible ethics complaint they might manipulate their data further, the concerned psychologists might appropriately have taken other action. Because the information in question was in the public domain and therefore available to anyone, if the concerned psychologists feared reprisals such as lawsuits, they could have submitted their complaint to an ethics panel anonymously.

D. Case Implications

Psychologists who have sound reasons for suspecting unethical behavior on the part of their colleagues have an obligation to pursue the possible violation, formally or informally. Such actions are a professional responsibility and serve to protect the well-being of clients and others who may be affected by problematic behavior of colleagues.

Raising ethical concerns is not a matter to be undertaken lightly. The concerned psychologist should be convinced that there is reasonable cause for suspecting unethical behavior. The complaint may first be raised directly with the affected party unless there is compelling reason not to do so.

Avoiding a confrontation, too often the response of choice for psychologists, or worse, damning the individual in a forum in which response is not possible (such as gossiping about the allegedly offending party with one's colleagues) is not a professional way to handle such matters. Depending on the situation, failing to take direct action may itself constitute an ethics violation.

Action should also be taken in a timely manner, preferably as soon after learning of the alleged violation as possible. Otherwise, statutes of limitations may apply, and ethics committees may not be able to address the issue if it is presented to them.

Case 59

Betraying a Confidence

A. Statement of the Problem

A psychologist, who published tests as a side business venture, invited an outside consultant, also a psychologist, to prepare a proposal for the development and validation of new test materials in a content area in which the consultant had established professional expertise and reputation. The psychologist had previously prepared tests for the individual. In prior work the terms of access to such materials had been noted, and the test developer assumed that those conditions applied to the new agreement. The consulting psychologist was contacted on a sole-source basis and was asked to prepare a multiyear proposal outlining work that would be completed for a negotiated contractual fee.

The psychologist expressed considerable interest in the project and agreed by phone to submit a proposal for the work. He then met with the first psychologist to discuss specifications for the project. In that meeting, he was given confidential marketing information on potential markets and marketing strategies as well as specifications for the testing products. This information was necessary for the psychologist to prepare an appropriate proposal and was noted to be confidential and proprietary.

One month later, not having heard from his colleague, the first psychologist contacted the consultant to ask about the status of the proposal. The psychologist told the director that in preparing to work on the proposal, he came to realize that it would be in his best economic interest to develop and market a test in this area on his own. This effort would capitalize on the psychologist's growing reputation in the content areas covered by the test.

The test developer expressed surprise and concern that the psychologist had not informed him of this new development. He indicated considerable unhappiness that the psychologist was reneging on his agreement to prepare a proposal for him and even greater concern that the proprietary information shared with the psychologist might, in the test developer's view, be unfairly used by the psychologist in his own test development efforts. Additionally, he explicitly stated that the information that had been shared with the psychologist was to be kept confidential and was not to be used in any manner by the psychologist or his firm.

The psychologist apologized for his delay in communicating his decision to the test publisher but noted that he had been busy with some other matters. He assured the psychologist that he would behave professionally in this situation and stated that he would immediately return the materials that had been sent to him. He indicated that in any event, due to the pressure of other commitments he had really not had time to look at the materials in detail.

A review of the psychologist's test products and subsequent marketing efforts revealed substantial similarities to the materials he had been given. It was clear to the test publisher that the psychologist had used information obtained in the meeting with the first psychologist for his own competitive advantage. When the test publisher objected to the psychologist, he explained that he had not used their marketing materials and that in any case he was legally free to compete as he saw fit with other providers of psychological services and products. The psychologist threatened to sue the psychologist, but because of the costs of litigation, no further action was taken on the claim.

B. Ethics Code Standards

Ethical Standard 1.17   Multiple Relationships

(a) ... A psychologist refrains from entering into or promising another personal, scientific, professional, financial, or other relationship with such persons if it appears likely that such a relationship reasonably might impair the psychologist's objectivity or otherwise interfere with the psychologist's effectively performing his or her functions as a psychologist, or might harm or exploit the other party.
(b) Likewise, whenever feasible, a psychologist refrains from taking on professional or scientific obligations when preexisting relationships would create a risk of such harm.

Ethical Standard 5.02   Maintaining Confidentiality

Psychologists have a primary obligation and take reasonable precautions to respect the confidentiality rights of those with whom they work or consult. . . .

C. Case Interpretation

The ethical issue raised by this case concerns not so much the decision to market a product or service in competition with a former client, as the manner in which the psychologist went about the process.

The opportunity to institutionalize expertise with a product is understandably highly valued by consulting psychologists. The consultant in this case appears initially not to have considered marketing test materials on his own and seemed pleased with the opportunity to propose work on a long-term project with his former client. It would appear that the idea to publish a competing product on his own occurred to him only after his meeting with his former client.

Of course a consultant is not forever barred from competing with a former client, particularly if there was no specific contract language to that effect (organizations often do have clients sign statements protecting proprietary information as a condition of engagement). The ethical concern in this case is not with the psychologist deciding not to follow through with his interest in proposing work to the test publisher. Rather, it is with his not having alerted the first psychologist that he had made a decision to market a product that would put him in direct competition with the test publisher and in his failure to communicate the decision immediately after it had been made. In effect, the psychologist unilaterally terminated his involvement with the former client and made no efforts to communicate this information or to protect his former client from exploitation.

Because the psychologist did not formally terminate the implied relationship he had with his former client, he in effect created a dual relationship by developing his own product that competed directly with the one the test publisher had wanted him to work on. Certainly he was in a compromising situation as soon as he decided to make his own product that would compete with that of the test publisher. The extent to which the psychologist actually made use of the testing company's information to develop or market his own tests is unknown but might cause the test publisher to have legitimate cause to initiate legal action if there were potential violations of the copyright laws.

Ethically, the psychologist should formally have terminated his relationship with the test publisher before becoming its competitor. As part of this process, the psychologist should have returned all notes and materials received from the testing corporation. Under the circumstances of his departure, the psychologist might also have referred the company to other competent personnel who might have been able to complete the assignment.

D. Case Implications

Ethical guidelines need not restrict competition. Psychologists, like any others, have the right to compete with others and to offer products or services in direct competition with others, including with former clients. Still, a psychologist has an obligation not to be deceptive or exploitative in his dealings with others and to keep colleagues informed when it becomes necessary to change the terms of, or to terminate, a professional relationship. Additionally, psychologists in their commercial dealings need to avoid dual relationships when they are harmful to one or more parties.

Above all, psychologists need carefully to think through their decisions and to anticipate the consequences and implications of their decisions. Clear communication with all affected parties when circumstances or commitments (including implied commitments) change is usually the best way to avoid unethical or otherwise unprofessional behavior.

When potential conflicted situations arise, the affected parties need to agree on the parameters to govern these situations. These agreements can be revised as circumstances dictate. The important ethical concern is that revisions to prior agreements not be made unilaterally and that all relevant parties be kept informed of changed circumstances as they occur.

Case 60

Psychologists as Employers of Other Psychologists

A. Statement of the Problem

The managers in a unit of a corporation were having difficulty working together. Their supervisor contacted the company's internal I/O psychologist for help in reducing the conflict. Because the psychologist was over-committed with her current assignments, she contracted for the services of another psychologist outside the firm to work with the managers on their identified concerns. Although this psychologist had no experience working in industry, he had an excellent and well-deserved reputation for his work in assessing and treating marital and family conflict. He also was eager to test the generalizability of his theories in industrial settings.

From the start of the work with the managers, there were negative comments about the consulting psychologist's approach and techniques. The complaints primarily concerned the use of seemingly irrelevant examples and a style that the managers felt talked down to them. Initially the comments were made informally to the consultant, but not long thereafter members of the management group working with him complained in writing about the way they were being treated and about the simplistic exercises in which they were asked to participate. Several managers eventually refused further participation even though the contract with the psychologist had 2 months remaining.

After hearing the informal complaints and receiving several written complaints, the internal psychologist consulted her boss, who was not a psychologist. As her supervisor recommended, she immediately terminated the contract by a letter stating that the consulting psychologist's services were no longer required. No meetings were held to review the reasons for the decision, nor was there any telephone contact about the situation. The psychologist's gate card was invalidated, and security guards were notified that the psychologist was not to be admitted to the plant.

After several unsuccessful attempts to reach the contracting psychologist by phone, the consulting psychologist demanded full payment for the contracted services and further challenged the decision to terminate the program midstream. When the payment was curtly refused, the consulting psychologist threatened to sue, at which point the company's legal advisor made the recommendation to pay the originally contracted amount to avoid litigation.

B. Ethics Code Standards

Ethical Standard 1.04   Boundaries of Competence

(a) Psychologists provide services ... only within the boundaries of their competence, based on their education, training, supervised experience, or appropriate professional experience.
(b) Psychologists provide services, teach, or conduct research in new areas or involving new techniques only after first undertaking appropriate study, training, supervision, and/or consultation from persons who are competent in those areas or techniques.

Ethical Standard 1.20   Consultations and Referrals

(a) Psychologists arrange for appropriate consultations and referrals based principally on the best interests of their ... clients....

Ethical Standard 1.22   Delegation to and Supervision of Subordinates

(a) Psychologists delegate to their employees, supervisees, and research assistants only those responsibilities that such persons can reasonably be expected to perform competently, on the basis of their education, training, or experience, either independently or with the level of supervision being provided.
(b) Psychologists provide proper training and supervision to their employees or supervisees and take reasonable steps to see that such persons perform services responsibly, competently, and ethically.

Ethical Standard 8.03   Conflicts Between Ethics and Organizational Demands

If the demands of an organization with which psychologists are affiliated conflict with this Ethics Code, psychologists clarify the nature of the conflict, make known their commitment to the Ethics Code, and to the extent feasible, seek to resolve the conflict in a way that permits the fullest adherence to the Ethics Code.

C. Case Interpretation

Professional competency (of both of the psychologists) is the central issue in this case. Both psychologists erred in their behavior.

The internal psychologist did not adequately consider the best interests of the psychologist's clients, the managers, in making the decision to contract for the services of a psychologist with no prior industrial experience. Regardless of the consulting psychologist's reputation in the area of conflict management, the absence of specific experience in industry should at least have raised the possibility that the needs of the managers might not be met by the particular approach to conflict management in which the contracted psychologist had specialized.

Under these circumstances, the contracting psychologist had a responsibility either to assure that the psychologist was competent in this new-to-him application or to monitor performance closely. When it became clear that the project was in trouble, the organizational psychologist needed to respond constructively to complaints about the quality of the intervention and to attempt to remediate the immediate difficulties. It is possible, for example, that the complaining managers had merely displaced their intradepartmental conflict onto the psychologist, who, as an "outsider," may have been a convenient target.

For his part, the contracted psychologist agreed to perform the requested services without recognizing that his inexperience in industrial application constituted a potential limitation. He should have arranged for appropriate supervision or consultation before accepting the assignment and should also have explored carefully with the hiring psychologist the limitations of his expertise and experience. When he became aware of the complaints, the psychologist should have taken immediate corrective action to modify his method and approach or to determine that the apparent conflict was actually reflecting important personal dynamics that could then have been used in the intervention. He should have immediately made the difficulties known to his supervising psychologist and modified his approach or gotten outside consultation to remediate the immediate situation. If, despite diligently making such efforts, the intervention still was the target of complaints, then the psychologist had an ethical obligation to terminate his involvement and refer the client to professionals with other approaches or methods.

D. Case Implications

Psychologists, especially those in large, complex organizations, often serve as employers or contractors of other psychologists. Whether in large firms or small ones, in such roles, psychologists have responsibility for assuring the quality of services they do not themselves provide. This implies the need both to select other professionals carefully and to monitor their performance closely, particularly in the early stages of a consulting relationship. Even well-earned professional reputations do not assure high quality of work in a different application or setting. In fact, assumptions of competence of a professional's reputation may cause a supervising psychologist not to attend properly to their managerial oversight responsibilities.

Clients, internal or external, reasonably expect that professional services will be competently delivered. When problems do arise it is important that they immediately be addressed, while it is still possible to make constructive changes. Preventative actions are also important. These can include reviewing a project's progress at selected intervals, calibrating expectations at the beginning and throughout the work, and establishing a mechanism for handling unanticipated problems. It is also important that the hiring psychologist legitimatize the obligation and expectation of the supervising psychologist to monitor and oversee the work of their colleagues.

Case 61 _____

When Romance Fails

A. Statement of the Problem

An I/O psychologist who was responsible for supervising I/O doctoral psychology student interns, after several months of intense involvement on a high-profile project, found himself romantically and sexually attracted to one of the female student interns. Through a mutual acquaintance, he learned that she was also attracted to him. The psychologist, who was only a year or two older than the intern, was a recent PhD graduate who had earned his doctorate at the intern's university. They had many common acquaintances and interests. After a few weeks of casual dating, they became involved in an intimate relationship.

They both knew that the dual relationship was potentially problematic but felt they were mature enough to handle any complications in a professional manner. Because others might not understand and because it might also have resulted in their not being able to work together, the psychologist advised the intern to keep the affair secret from their work and university-based colleagues. Both parties agreed that their work productivity was being enhanced because of the close contact they had with one another in both their work and social lives.

Over time, the romantic relationship soured, and the supervisor stated that it would be best for them to end the affair. The student intern was devastated by this loss, and she became even more upset as she discovered she was now in the position of having to serve her internship under the supervision of one who was increasingly cold, obviously distanced, and who was becoming more and more critical of her work, which, previously, he had praised as being exceptionally good. Both her internship and school-work suffered with her emotional distress. When the intern accused her boss of having taken unfair and inappropriate advantage of her, he reminded her that the affair had been entirely mutually consensual. He also stated that because he was not a licensed psychologist (although he was a member of several professional organizations, including the APA and the SIOP) the psychology ethics code did not apply to him. He suggested that it would be best for all concerned if she transferred to another business unit to complete her internship. Ultimately, she did transfer out of his section and completed the internship in a satisfactory manner.

B. Ethics Code Standards

Ethical Standard 1.14   Avoiding Harm

Psychologists take reasonable steps to avoid harming their ... students, and others with whom they work, and to minimize harm where it is foreseeable and unavoidable.

Ethical Standard 1.17   Multiple Relationships

(a) ... Psychologists must always be sensitive to the potential harmful effects of other contacts on their work and on those persons with whom they deal. A psychologist refrains from entering into or promising another personal, scientific, professional, financial, or other relationship with such persons if it appears likely that such a relationship reasonably might impair the psychologist's objectivity or otherwise interfere with the psychologist's effectively performing his or her function as a psychologist, or might harm or exploit the other party.

Ethical Standard 1.19   Exploitative Relationships

(b) Psychologists do not engage in sexual relationships with students or supervisees in training over whom the psychologist has evaluative or direct authority, because such relationships are so likely to impair judgment or be exploitative.

C. Case Interpretation

The psychologist's behavior in this case was unethical from a number of perspectives. The psychologist in this case should have refrained from engaging in a romantic relationship with his supervisee; that behavior violated the Ethical Standards. The intern should also have recognized the dangers inherent in any romance with her supervisor. Once the unethical sexual engagement did begin, the psychologist should at the least have transferred his supervisory responsibilities to another qualified I/O psychologist.

In his supervisory position, the psychologist clearly had power and authority over the student trainee. As such, it was his responsibility to avoid potential conflict and harm. By continuing to supervise the intern after becoming romantically involved with her, the psychologist allowed himself to be part of a dual relationship, and thus established a potentially exploitative situation. The fact that he asked his partner to keep the relationship secret contributes to the perception of its illicit nature. The failure of the personal relationship eventually led to an unsatisfactory work environment for the student intern, whose work and personal life suffered as the result of this experience. Laws and institutional rules may raise additional problems, such as other students or staff who become aware of the relationship, or the intern, after the relationship ended, experiencing the setting as a hostile workplace environment.

The psychologist also erred in his assertion that he was not subject to ethics code because he was not a licensed psychologist. Membership in professional organizations, such as APA and SIOP, commits members to adhere to the Ethics Code. In addition, the Ethical Principles of Psychologists and Code of Conduct (APA, 1992) state that "psychologists and students, whether or not they are APA members, should be aware that the Ethics Code may be applied to them by state psychology boards, courts, or other public bodies" (p. 1598).

D. Case Implications

Most organizations and universities have adopted policies that seek to prevent various forms of sexual impropriety and to avoid hostile work environments. Typically, these policies provide sanctions when company policy or the law have been violated. However, sexual exploitation can occur in more subtle forms, even when a relationship appears to be a consensual one between well-informed adults.

It is understandable that work and school settings provide opportunities for new social relationships. The difficulty with such relationships arises when professionals attempt to engage in multiple relationships, such as with students, supervisees, and clients, with whom they have other, prior and ongoing relationships. Psychologists must always be sensitive to the potentially harmful effects of dual or multiple relationships. The likelihood for harm increases whenever there exists a power differential between parties in a relationship. I/O psychologists, like any others, must guard against using their power inappropriately to serve their own self-interests.

Psychologists in supervisory positions need also to consider the impact of a dual relationship on others with whom they work. Whether or not the perception is accurate, favoritism is likely to be attributed to those in such relationships. I/O psychologists must consider their professional obligations to others as supervisors, educators, and leaders. When a potential conflict arises between personal and professional relationships, psychologists should carefully consider the implications of multiple relationships before deciding how to proceed.

Postscript

With the passage of time, the modification of ethics codes, and new forms of professional practice, casebooks such as these need revision. As you encounter ideas for new cases, or for revisions of old ones, please help SIOP prepare the next edition of the casebook.

Please send your suggested cases, ideas for new cases, or recommended new cases to SIOP's Executive Offices, which will collect these for use in preparation of the next edition. Address correspondence to

Ethics Casebook Revision
SIOP Administrative Office
745 Haskins Rd., Suite D
P.O. Box 87
Bowling Green, OH 43402-0087

References

American Psychological Association. (1992). Ethical principles of psychologists and code of conduct. *American Psychologist, 47,* 1597–1611. [The APA Ethical Principles are on-line at the APA website and may be found at http://www.apa.org/ethics/code.html]

Lowman, R. L. (1985). *Casebook on ethics and standards for the practice of psychology in organizations.* Bowling Green, OH: Society for Industrial and Organizational Psychology.

Society for Industrial and Organizational Psychology. (1987). *Principles for the validation and use of personnel selection procedures.* Bowling Green, OH: Author.

Selected Bibliography

A recent psychology literature search of the term *ethics* found more than 10,000 citations. The following list of resources for suggested additional readings is necessarily selective. This partial and eclectic list is intended to assist the serious reader wanting to learn more about ethical issues related to the practice of I/O psychology.

Allegretti, C. L., & Frederick, J. (1995). A model for thinking critically about ethical issues. *Teaching of Psychology, 22,* 46–48.

American Psychological Association, Ethics Committee. (1995). Report of the Ethics Committee, 1994. *American Psychologist, 50,* 706–713.

American Psychological Association, Ethics Committee. (1996). Report of the Ethics Committee, 1995. *American Psychologist, 51,* 1279–1286.

American Psychological Association, Ethics Committee. (1996). Rules and procedures: Ethics Committee of the American Psychological Association. *American Psychologist, 51,* 529–548.

Baehr, M. E., Jones, J. W., & Nerad, A. J. (1993). Psychological correlates of business ethics orientation in executives. *Journal of Business and Psychology, 7,* 291–308.

Bersoff, D. N. (Ed.). (1994). *Ethical conflicts in psychology.* Washington, DC: American Psychological Association.

Bersoff, D. N. (1994). Explicit ambiguity: The 1992 ethics code as an oxymoron. *Professional Psychology Research and Practice, 25,* 382–387.

Brown, M. T. (1990). *Working ethics: Strategies for decision making and organizational responsibility.* San Francisco: Jossey-Bass.

Butcher, J. N., & Pope, K. S. (1993). Seven issues in conducting forensic assessments: Ethical responsibilities in light of new standards and new tests. *Ethics and Behavior, 3,* 267–288.

Canter, M. B., Bennett, B. E., Jones, S. E., & Nagy, T. F. (1994). *Ethics for psychologists: A commentary on the APA Ethics Code.* Washington, DC: American Psychological Association.

Carkenord, D. M. (1996). A group exercise to explore employee ethics in business-related psychology courses. *Teaching of Psychology, 23,* 100–102.

Carroll, S. J., & Gannon, M. J. (1997). *Ethical dimensions of international management.* Thousand Oaks, CA: Sage.

Catano, V. M. (1994). Application of the CPA code of ethics: Towards integrating the science and practice of psychology. *Canadian Psychology, 35,* 224–228.

Clark, R. W., & Lattal, A. D. (1993). *Workplace ethics: Winning the integrity revolution.* Lanham, MD: Rowman & Littlefield.

Crossen, B. R. (1993). Managing employee unethical behavior without invading individual privacy. *Journal of Business and Psychology, 8,* 227–243.

Dana, R. H. (1994). Testing and assessment ethics for all persons: Beginning an agenda. *American Psychologist, 49,* 659–666.

Daniel, L. G., Elliott, H., Florence, E., & DuFrene, D. (1997). The ethical issues rating scale: An instrument for measuring ethical orientation of college students toward various business practices. *Educational and Psychological Measurement, 57,* 515–526.

Deetz, S. (1985). Ethical considerations in cultural research in organizations. In P. J. Frost & L. F. Moore (Eds.), *Organizational culture* (pp. 253–269). Thousand Oaks, CA: Sage.

Eyde, L. D., & Kowal, D. M. (1987). Computerised test interpretation services: Ethical and professional concerns regarding U.S. producers and users. *Applied Psychology: An International Review, 36,* 401–417.

Eyde, L. D., & Quaintance, M. K. (1988). Ethical issues and cases in the practice of personnel psychology. *Professional Psychology Research and Practice, 19,* 148–154.

Eyde, L. D., Robertson, G. J., Krug, S. E., Moreland, K. L., Robertson, A. G., Shewan, C. M., Harrison, P. L., Porch, B. E., Hammer, A. L., & Primoff, E. S. (1993). *Responsible test use: Case studies for assessing human behavior.* Washington, DC: American Psychological Association.

Finegan, J., & Theriault, C. (1997). The relationship between personal values and the perception of the corporation's code of ethics. *Journal of Applied Social Psychology, 27,* 708–724.

Flescher, L. (1991). Ethical implications in screening for ethics violations. *Ethics and Behavior, 1,* 259–271.

Gellermann, W., Frankel, M. S., Ladenson, R. F. (1990). *Values and ethics in organization and human systems development: Responding to dilemmas in professional life.* San Francisco: Jossey-Bass.

Germeroth, D. (1994). Guidelines for the ethical conduct of organizational development agents. *International Journal of Organizational Analysis, 2,* 117–135.

Goodstein, L. D. (1984). Ethical pitfalls for managers. *Professional Psychology Research and Practice, 15,* 749–757.

Gorlin, R. A. (Ed.). (1990). *Codes of professional responsibility* (2nd ed.). Washington, DC: Bureau of National Affairs, Inc.

Gray, R. H. (1990). Business ethics and organisational change. *Leadership and Organization Development Journal, 11,* 12–21.

Haney, W., & Madaus, G. (1991). The evolution of ethical and technical standards for testing. In R. K. Hambleton & J. N. Zaal (Eds.), *Advances in educational and psychological testing: Theory and applications* (pp. 395–425). Boston: Kluwer Academic Publishers.

Harvey, S. (1994). Application of the CPA Code of Ethics in planning field research: An organizational case. *Canadian Psychology, 35,* 204–219.

Jacques, P. (1991). Legal and ethical issues in psychological assessment. In C. P. Hansen & K. A. Conrad (Eds.), *A handbook of psychological assessment in business* (pp. 313–330). New York: Quorum Books.

Hopkins, W. E. (1997). *Ethical dimensions of diversity.* Thousand Oaks, CA: Sage.

Jones, S. E. (1993). Determination of authorship credits. *Psychological Science, 4,* 271.

Jones, T. M. (1991). Ethical decision making by individuals in organizations: An issue-contingent model. *Academy of Management Review, 16,* 366–395.

Kline, T. J. B. (1994). Using the CPA Code of Ethics in I/O psychology. *Canadian Psychology, 35,* 220–223.

Kobrick, F. R., Rodwin, M. A., & VandenBos, G. R. (1993). Inside information. *Ethics and Behavior, 3,* 135–147.

Lee, S. S., & Rosen, E. A. (1984). Employee counseling services: Ethical dilemmas. *Personnel and Guidance Journal, 62,* 276–280.

London, M., & Bray, D. W. (1980). Ethical issues in testing and evaluation for personnel decisions. *American Psychologist, 35,* 890–901.

Lowman, R. L. (1986). The ethical practice of consultation: Not an impossible dream. *The Counseling Psychologist, 13,* 466–472.

Lowman, R. L. (1990). Comments on organization development cases. In W. Gellerman, M. S. Frankel, & R. F. Ladenson (Eds.), *Values and ethics in organization and human systems development: Responding to dilemmas in professional life* (pp. 244–250; 454–456). San Francisco: Jossey-Bass.

Lowman, R. L. (1991). Ethical issues in applying psychology in organizations. In J. J. Jones, B. P. Steffy, & D. W. Bray (Eds.), *Applying psychology in organizations* (pp. 40–47). Lexington, MA: Lexington Books.

Lowman, R. L. (1993). An ethics code for I/O psychology: For what purpose and at what cost? *The Industrial/Organizational Psychologist, 31,* 90–92.

Lowman, R. L. (1996). Ethical issues and dilemmas in fair employment strategy. In R. S. Barrett (Ed.), *Fair employment strategies in human resource management* (pp. 12–19). Westport, CT: Quorum Books/Greenwood Publishing Co.

Melton, G. B. (1988). Must researchers share their data? *Law and Human Behavior, 12,* 159–162.

Mirvis, P. H., & Seashore, S. E. (1979). Being ethical in organizational research. *American Psychologist, 34,* 766–780.

National Academies of Sciences & Engineering, and Institute of Medicine. (1995). *On being a scientist: Responsible conduct in research* (2nd ed.). Washington, DC: Author.

Orr, P. (1997). Psychology impaired? *Professional Psychology Research and Practice, 28,* 293–296.

Payne, S. L., & Giacalone, R. A. (1990). Social psychological approaches to the perception of ethical dilemmas. *Human Relations, 43,* 649–665.

Pope, K. S., & Vetter, V. A. (1992). Ethical dilemmas encountered by members of the American Psychological Association: A national survey. *American Psychologist, 47,* 397–411.

Pryor, R. G. (1989). Conflicting responsibilities: A case study of an ethical dilemma for psychologists working in organisations. *Australian Psychologist, 24,* 293–305.

Pryzwansky, W. B., & Wendt, R. N. (1987). *Psychology as a profession: Foundations of practice.* Elmsford, NY: Pergamon Press.

Rhodeback, M., Wen, B., & White, L. P. (1990). Ethical consideration in organization development: An empirical approach. *Organizational Development Journal, 8,* 40–49.

Rodgers, R. (1992). Investigating psychology's taboo: The ethics of editing. *Ethics and Behavior, 2,* 253–261.

Seashore, S. E. (1978). Plagiarism, credit assignment, and ownership of data. *Professional Psychology, 9,* 719–722.

Shea, C., & Bond, T. (1997). Ethical issues for counseling in organizations. In M. Carroll & M. Walton (Eds.), *Handbook of counselling in organizations* (pp. 187–205). Thousand Oaks, CA: Sage.

Sieber, J. E. (1994). Will the new code help researchers to be more ethical? *Professional Psychology Research and Practice, 25,* 369–375.

Stanley, B. H., Sieber, J. E., & Melton, G. B. (Eds.). (1996). *Research ethics: A psychological approach.* Lincoln, NE: University of Nebraska Press.

Sugarman, L. (1992). Ethical issues in counselling at work. *British Journal of Guidance and Counselling, 20,* 64–74.

Tannenbaum, S. I., Greene, V. J., & Glickman, A. S. (1989). The ethical reasoning process in an organizational consulting situation. *Professional Psychology Research and Practice, 20,* 229–235.

Tranel, D. (1994). The release of psychological data to nonexperts: Ethical and legal considerations. *Professional Psychology Research and Practice, 25,* 33–38.

Trevino, L. K., & Ball, G. A. (1992). The social implications of punishing unethical behavior: Observers' cognitive and affective reactions. *Journal of Management, 18,* 751–768.

Trevino, L. K., & Victor, B. (1992). Peer reporting of unethical behavior: A social context perspective. *Academy of Management Journal, 35,* 38–64.

Trevino, L. K., & Youngblood, S. A. (1990). Bad apples in bad barrels: A causal analysis of ethical decision-making behavior. *Journal of Applied Psychology, 75,* 378–385.

White, L. P., Wooten, K. C. (1988). O.D. ethics: A developmental model. *Organization Development Journal, 6,* 13–17.

Appendix

Ethical Principles of Psychologists and Code of Conduct

CONTENTS

Introduction

The American Psychological Association's (APA's) Ethical Principles of Psychologists and Code of Conduct (hereinafter referred to as the Ethics Code) consists of an Introduction, a Preamble, six General Principles (A–F), and specific Ethical Standards. The Introduction discusses the intent, organization, procedural considerations, and scope of application of the Ethics Code. The Preamble and General Principles are *aspirational* goals to guide psychologists toward the highest ideals of psychology. Although the Preamble and General Principles are not themselves enforceable rules, they should be considered by psychologists in arriving at an ethical course of action and may be considered by ethics bodies in interpreting the Ethical Standards. The Ethical Standards set forth *enforceable* rules for conduct as psychologists. Most of the Ethical Standards are written broadly, in order to apply to psychologists in varied roles, although the application of an Ethical Standard may vary depending on the context. The Ethical Standards are not exhaustive. The fact that a given conduct

Reprinted from *American Psychologist*, Vol. 47, pp. 1597–1611. Copyright 1992 by the American Psychological Association.

This version of the APA Ethics Code was adopted by the American Psychological Association's Council of Representatives during its meeting, August 13 and 16, 1992, and is effective beginning December 1, 1992. Inquiries concerning the substance or interpretation of the APA Ethics Code should be addressed to the Director, Office of Ethics, American Psychological Association, 750 First Street, NE, Washington, DC 20002-4242.

This Code will be used to adjudicate complaints brought concerning alleged conduct occurring on or after the effective date. Complaints regarding conduct occurring prior to the effective date will be adjudicated on the basis of the version of the Code that was in effect at the time the conduct occurred, except that no provisions repealed in June 1989 will be enforced even if an earlier version contains the provision. The Ethics Code will undergo continuing review and study for future revisions; comments on the Code may be sent to the above address.

The APA has previously published its Ethical Standards as follows:

American Psychological Association. (1953). *Ethical standards of psychologists*. Washington, DC: Author.

American Psychological Association. (1958). Standards of ethical behavior for psychologists. *American Psychologist, 13*, 268–271.

American Psychological Association. (1963). Ethical standards of psychologists. *American Psychologist, 18*, 56–60.

American Psychological Association. (1968). Ethical standards of psychologists. *American Psychologist, 23*, 357–361.

American Psychological Association. (1977, March). Ethical standards of psychologists. *APA Monitor*, pp. 22–23.

American Psychological Association. (1979). *Ethical standards of psychologists*. Washington, DC: Author.

American Psychological Association. (1981). Ethical principles of psychologists. *American Psychologist, 36*, 633–638.

American Psychological Association. (1990). Ethical principles of psychologists (Amended June 2, 1989). *American Psychologist, 4*, 390–395.

Request copies of the APA's Ethical Principles of Psychologists and Code of Conduct from the APA Order Department, 750 First Street, NE, Washington, DC 20002-4242, or phone (202) 336-5510.

is not specifically addressed by the Ethics Code does not mean that it is necessarily either ethical or unethical.

Membership in the APA commits members to adhere to the APA Ethics Code and to the rules and procedures used to implement it. Psychologists and students, whether or not they are APA members, should be aware that the Ethics Code may be applied to them by state psychology boards, courts, or other public bodies.

This Ethics Code applies only to psychologists' work-related activities, that is, activities that are part of the psychologists' scientific and professional functions or that are psychological in nature. It includes the clinical or counseling practice of psychology, research, teaching, supervision of trainees, development of assessment instruments, conducting assessments, educational counseling, organizational consulting, social intervention, administration, and other activities as well. These work-related activities can be distinguished from the purely private conduct of a psychologist, which ordinarily is not within the purview of the Ethics Code.

The Ethics Code is intended to provide standards of professional conduct that can be applied by the APA and by other bodies that choose to adopt them. Whether or not a psychologist has violated the Ethics Code does not by itself determine whether he or she is legally liable in a court action, whether a contract is enforceable, or whether other legal consequences occur. These results are based on legal rather than ethical rules. However, compliance with or violation of the Ethics Code may be admissible as evidence in some legal proceedings, depending on the circumstances.

In the process of making decisions regarding their professional behavior, psychologists must consider this Ethics Code, in addition to applicable laws and psychology board regulations. If the Ethics Code establishes a higher standard of conduct than is required by law, psychologists must meet the higher ethical standard. If the Ethics Code standard appears to conflict with the requirements of law, then psychologists make known their commitment to the Ethics Code and take steps to resolve the conflict in a responsible manner. If neither law nor the Ethics Code resolves an issue, psychologists should consider other professional materials[1] and the dic-

---

[1]Professional materials that are most helpful in this regard are guidelines and standards that have been adopted or endorsed by professional psychological organizations. Such guidelines and standards, whether adopted by the American Psychological Association (APA) or its Divisions, are not enforceable as such by this Ethics Code, but are of educative value to psychologists, courts, and professional bodies. Such materials include, but are not limited to, the APA's *General Guidelines for Providers of Psychological Services* (1987), *Specialty Guidelines for the Delivery of Services by Clinical Psychologists, Counseling Psychologists, Industrial/Organizational Psychologists, and School Psychologists* (1981), *Guidelines for Computer Based Tests and Interpretations* (1987), *Standards for Educational and Psychological Testing* (1985), *Ethical Principles in the Conduct of Research With Human Participants* (1982), *Guidelines for Ethical Conduct in the Care and Use of Animals* (1986), *Guidelines for Providers of Psychological Services to Ethnic, Linguistic, and Culturally Diverse Populations* (1990), and *Publication Manual of the American Psychological Association* (3rd ed., 1983). Materials not adopted by APA as a whole include the APA Division 41 (Forensic Psychology)/American Psychology–Law Society's *Specialty Guidelines for Forensic Psychologists* (1991).

tates of their own conscience, as well as seek consultation with others within the field when this is practical.

The procedures for filing, investigating, and resolving complaints of unethical conduct are described in the current Rules and Procedures of the APA Ethics Committee. The actions that APA may take for violations of the Ethics Code include actions such as reprimand, censure, termination of APA membership, and referral of the matter to other bodies. Complainants who seek remedies such as monetary damages in alleging ethical violations by a psychologist must resort to private negotiation, administrative bodies, or the courts. Actions that violate the Ethics Code may lead to the imposition of sanctions on a psychologist by bodies other than APA, including state psychological associations, other professional groups, psychology boards, other state or federal agencies, and payors for health services. In addition to actions for violation of the Ethics Code, the APA Bylaws provide that APA may take action against a member after his or her conviction of a felony, expulsion or suspension from an affiliated state psychological association, or suspension or loss of licensure.

Preamble

Psychologists work to develop a valid and reliable body of scientific knowledge based on research. They may apply that knowledge to human behavior in a variety of contexts. In doing so, they perform many roles, such as researcher, educator, diagnostician, therapist, supervisor, consultant, administrator, social interventionist, and expert witness. Their goal is to broaden knowledge of behavior and, where appropriate, to apply it pragmatically to improve the condition of both the individual and society. Psychologists respect the central importance of freedom of inquiry and expression in research, teaching, and publication. They also strive to help the public in developing informed judgments and choices concerning human behavior. This Ethics Code provides a common set of values upon which psychologists build their professional and scientific work.

This Code is intended to provide both the general principles and the decision rules to cover most situations encountered by psychologists. It has as its primary goal the welfare and protection of the individuals and groups with whom psychologists work. It is the individual responsibility of each psychologist to aspire to the highest possible standards of conduct. Psychologists respect and protect human and civil rights, and do not knowingly participate in or condone unfair discriminatory practices.

The development of a dynamic set of ethical standards for a psychologist's work-related conduct requires a personal commitment to a lifelong effort to act ethically; to encourage ethical behavior by students, supervisees, employees, and colleagues, as appropriate; and to consult with others, as needed, concerning ethical problems. Each psychologist supplements, but does not violate, the Ethics Code's values and rules on the basis of guidance drawn from personal values, culture, and experience.

General Principles

Principle A: Competence

Psychologists strive to maintain high standards of competence in their work. They recognize the boundaries of their particular competencies and the limitations of their expertise. They provide only those services and use only those techniques for which they are qualified by education, training, or experience. Psychologists are cognizant of the fact that the competencies required in serving, teaching, and/or studying groups of people vary with the distinctive characteristics of those groups. In those areas in which recognized professional standards do not yet exist, psychologists exercise careful judgment and take appropriate precautions to protect the welfare of those with whom they work. They maintain knowledge of relevant scientific and professional information related to the services they render, and they recognize the need for ongoing education. Psychologists make appropriate use of scientific, professional, technical, and administrative resources.

Principle B: Integrity

Psychologists seek to promote integrity in the science, teaching, and practice of psychology. In these activities psychologists are honest, fair, and respectful of others. In describing or reporting their qualifications, services, products, fees, research, or teaching, they do not make statements that are false, misleading, or deceptive. Psychologists strive to be aware of their own belief systems, values, needs, and limitations and the effect of these on their work. To the extent feasible, they attempt to clarify for relevant parties the roles they are performing and to function appropriately in accordance with those roles. Psychologists avoid improper and potentially harmful dual relationships.

Principle C: Professional and Scientific Responsibility

Psychologists uphold professional standards of conduct, clarify their professional roles and obligations, accept appropriate responsibility for their behavior, and adapt their methods to the needs of different populations. Psychologists consult with, refer to, or cooperate with other professionals and institutions to the extent needed to serve the best interests of their patients, clients, or other recipients of their services. Psychologists' moral standards and conduct are personal matters to the same degree as is true for any other person, except as psychologists' conduct may compromise their professional responsibilities or reduce the public's trust in psychology and psychologists. Psychologists are concerned about the ethical compliance of their colleagues' scientific and professional conduct. When appropriate, they consult with colleagues in order to prevent or avoid unethical conduct.

Principle D: Respect for People's Rights and Dignity

Psychologists accord appropriate respect to the fundamental rights, dignity, and worth of all people. They respect the rights of individuals to privacy, confidentiality, self-determination, and autonomy, mindful that legal and other obligations may lead to inconsistency and conflict with the exercise of these rights. Psychologists are aware of cultural, individual, and role differences, including those due to age, gender, race, ethnicity, national origin, religion, sexual orientation, disability, language, and socioeconomic status. Psychologists try to eliminate the effect on their work of biases based on those factors, and they do not knowingly participate in or condone unfair discriminatory practices.

Principle E: Concern for Others' Welfare

Psychologists seek to contribute to the welfare of those with whom they interact professionally. In their professional actions, psychologists weigh the welfare and rights of their patients or clients, students, supervisees, human research participants, and other affected persons, and the welfare of animal subjects of research. When conflicts occur among psychologists' obligations or concerns, they attempt to resolve these conflicts and to perform their roles in a responsible fashion that avoids or minimizes harm. Psychologists are sensitive to real and ascribed differences in power between themselves and others, and they do not exploit or mislead other people during or after professional relationships.

Principle F: Social Responsibility

Psychologists are aware of their professional and scientific responsibilities to the community and the society in which they work and live. They apply and make public their knowledge of psychology in order to contribute to human welfare. Psychologists are concerned about and work to mitigate the causes of human suffering. When undertaking research, they strive to advance human welfare and the science of psychology. Psychologists try to avoid misuse of their work. Psychologists comply with the law and encourage the development of law and social policy that serve the interests of their patients and clients and the public. They are encouraged to contribute a portion of their professional time for little or no personal advantage.

Ethical Standards

1. *General Standards*

These General Standards are potentially applicable to the professional and scientific activities of all psychologists.

1.01 Applicability of the Ethics Code

The activity of a psychologist subject to the Ethics Code may be reviewed under these Ethical Standards only if the activity is part of his or her work-related functions or the activity is psychological in nature. Personal activities having no connection to or effect on psychological roles are not subject to the Ethics Code.

1.02 Relationship of Ethics and Law

If psychologists' ethical responsibilities conflict with law, psychologists make known their commitment to the Ethics Code and take steps to resolve the conflict in a responsible manner.

1.03 Professional and Scientific Relationship

Psychologists provide diagnostic, therapeutic, teaching, research, supervisory, consultative, or other psychological services only in the context of a defined professional or scientific relationship or role. (See also Standards 2.01, Evaluation, Diagnosis, and Interventions in Professional Context, and 7.02, Forensic Assessments.)

1.04 Boundaries of Competence

(a) Psychologists provide services, teach, and conduct research only within the boundaries of their competence, based on their education, training, supervised experience, or appropriate professional experience.

(b) Psychologists provide services, teach, or conduct research in new areas or involving new techniques only after first undertaking appropriate study, training, supervision, and/or consultation from persons who are competent in those areas or techniques.

(c) In those emerging areas in which generally recognized standards for preparatory training do not yet exist, psychologists nevertheless take reasonable steps to ensure the competence of their work and to protect patients, clients, students, research participants, and others from harm.

1.05 Maintaining Expertise

Psychologists who engage in assessment, therapy, teaching, research, organizational consulting, or other professional activities maintain a reasonable level of awareness of current scientific and professional information in their fields of activity, and undertake ongoing efforts to maintain competence in the skills they use.

1.06 Basis for Scientific and Professional Judgments

Psychologists rely on scientifically and professionally derived knowledge when making scientific or professional judgments or when engaging in scholarly or professional endeavors.

1.07 Describing the Nature and Results of Psychological Services

(a) When psychologists provide assessment, evaluation, treatment, counseling, supervision, teaching, consultation, research, or other psychological services to an individual, a group, or an organization, they provide, using language that is reasonably understandable to the recipient of those services, appropriate information beforehand about the nature of such services and appropriate information later about results and consultations. (See also Standard 2.09, Explaining Assessment Results.)

(b) If psychologists will be precluded by law or by organizational roles from providing such information to particular individuals or groups, they so inform those individuals or groups at the outset of the service.

1.08 Human Differences

Where differences of age, gender, race, ethnicity, national origin, religion, sexual orientation, disability, language, or socioeconomic status significantly affect psychologists' work concerning particular individuals or groups, psychologists obtain the training, experience, consultation, or supervision necessary to ensure the competence of their services, or they make appropriate referrals.

1.09 Respecting Others

In their work-related activities, psychologists respect the rights of others to hold values, attitudes, and opinions that differ from their own.

1.10 Nondiscrimination

In their work-related activities, psychologists do not engage in unfair discrimination based on age, gender, race, ethnicity, national origin, religion, sexual orientation, disability, socioeconomic status, or any basis proscribed by law.

1.11 Sexual Harassment

(a) Psychologists do not engage in sexual harassment. Sexual harassment is sexual solicitation, physical advances, or verbal or nonverbal conduct that is sexual in nature, that occurs in connection with the psychologist's activities or roles as a psychologist, and that either: (1) is unwelcome, is offensive, or creates a hostile workplace environment, and the psychologist knows or is told this; or (2) is sufficiently severe or intense to be abusive to a reasonable person in the context. Sexual harassment can consist of a single intense or severe act or of multiple persistent or pervasive acts.

(b) Psychologists accord sexual-harassment complaints and respondents dignity and respect. Psychologists do not participate in denying a person academic admittance or advancement, employment, tenure, or promotion, based solely upon their having made, or their being the subject of, sexual-harassment charges. This does not preclude taking action based upon the outcome of such proceedings or consideration of other appropriate information.

1.12 Other Harassment

Psychologists do not knowingly engage in behavior that is harassing or demeaning to persons with whom they interact in their work based on factors such as those persons' age, gender, race, ethnicity, national origin, religion, sexual orientation, disability, language, or socioeconomic status.

1.13 Personal Problems and Conflicts

(a) Psychologists recognize that their personal problems and conflicts may interfere with their effectiveness. Accordingly, they refrain from undertaking an activity when they know or should know that their personal problems are likely to lead to harm to a patient, client, colleague, student, research participant, or other person to whom they may owe a professional or scientific obligation.

(b) In addition, psychologists have an obligation to be alert to signs of, and to obtain assistance for, their personal problems at an early stage, in order to prevent significantly impaired performance.

(c) When psychologists become aware of personal problems that may interfere with their performing work-related duties adequately, they take appropriate measures, such as obtaining professional consultation or assistance, and determine whether they should limit, suspend, or terminate their work-related duties.

1.14 Avoiding Harm

Psychologists take reasonable steps to avoid harming their patients or clients, research participants, students, and others with whom they work, and to minimize harm where it is foreseeable and unavoidable.

1.15 Misuse of Psychologists' Influence

Because psychologists' scientific and professional judgments and actions may affect the lives of others, they are alert to and guard against personal, financial, social, organizational, or political factors that might lead to misuse of their influence.

1.16 Misuse of Psychologists' Work

(a) Psychologists do not participate in activities in which it appears likely that their skills or data will be misused by others, unless corrective mechanisms are available. (See also Standard 7.04, Truthfulness and Candor.)

(b) If psychologists learn of misuse or misrepresentation of their work, they take reasonable steps to correct or minimize the misuse or misrepresentation.

1.17 Multiple Relationships

(a) In many communities and situations, it may not be feasible or reasonable for psychologists to avoid social or other nonprofessional contacts with persons such as patients, clients, students, supervisees, or research participants. Psychologists must always be sensitive to the potential harmful effects of other contacts on their work and on those persons with whom they deal. A psychologist refrains from entering into or promising another personal, scientific, professional, financial, or other relationship with such persons if it appears likely that such a relationship reasonably might impair the psychologist's objectivity or otherwise interfere with the psychologist's effectively performing his or her function as a psychologist, or might harm or exploit the other party.

(b) Likewise, whenever feasible, a psychologist refrains from taking on professional or scientific obligations when preexisting relationships would create a risk of such harm.

(c) If a psychologist finds that, due to unforeseen factors, a potentially harmful multiple relationship has arisen, the psychologist attempts to resolve it with due regard for the best interests of the affected person and maximal compliance with the Ethics Code.

1.18 Barter (With Patients or Clients)

Psychologists ordinarily refrain from accepting goods, services, or other nonmonetary remuneration from patients or clients in return for psychological services because such arrangements create inherent potential for conflicts, exploitation, and distortion of the professional relationship. A psychologist may participate in bartering only if (1) it is not clinically contraindicated, and (2) the relationship is not exploitative. (See also

Standards 1.17, Multiple Relationships, and 1.25, Fees and Financial Arrangements.)

1.19 Exploitative Relationships

(a) Psychologists do not exploit persons over whom they have supervisory, evaluative, or other authority such as students, supervisees, employees, research participants, and clients or patients. (See also Standards 4.05–4.07 regarding sexual involvement with clients or patients.)

(b) Psychologists do not engage in sexual relationships with students or supervisees in training over whom the psychologist has evaluative or direct authority, because such relationships are so likely to impair judgment or be exploitative.

1.20 Consultations and Referrals

(a) Psychologists arrange for appropriate consultations and referrals based principally on the best interests of their patients or clients, with appropriate consent, and subject to other relevant considerations, including applicable law and contractual obligations. (See also Standards 5.01, Discussing the Limits of Confidentiality, and 5.06, Consultations.)

(b) When indicated and professionally appropriate, psychologists cooperate with other professionals in order to serve their patients or clients effectively and appropriately.

(c) Psychologists' referral practices are consistent with law.

1.21 Third-Party Requests for Services

(a) When a psychologist agrees to provide services to a person or entity at the request of a third party, the psychologist clarifies to the extent feasible, at the outset of the service, the nature of the relationship with each party. This clarification includes the role of the psychologist (such as therapist, organizational consultant, diagnostician, or expert witness), the probable uses of the services provided or the information obtained, and the fact that there may be limits to confidentiality.

(b) If there is a foreseeable risk of the psychologist's being called upon to perform conflicting roles because of the involvement of a third party, the psychologist clarifies the nature and direction of his or her responsibilities, keeps all parties appropriately informed as matters develop, and resolves the situation in accordance with this Ethics Code.

1.22 Delegation to and Supervision of Subordinates

(a) Psychologists delegate to their employees, supervisees, and research assistants only those responsibilities that such persons can reasonably be expected to perform competently, on the basis of their education, training, or experience, either independently or with the level of supervision being provided.

(b) Psychologists provide proper training and supervision to their employees or supervisees and take reasonable steps to see that such persons perform services responsibly, competently, and ethically.

(c) If institutional policies, procedures, or practices prevent fulfillment of this obligation, psychologists attempt to modify their role or to correct the situation to the extent feasible.

1.23 Documentation of Professional and Scientific Work

(a) Psychologists appropriately document their professional and scientific work in order to facilitate provision of services later by them or by other professionals, to ensure accountability, and to meet other requirements of institutions or the law.

(b) When psychologists have reason to believe that records of their professional services will be used in legal proceedings involving recipients of or participants in their work, they have a responsibility to create and maintain documentation in the kind of detail and quality that would be consistent with reasonable scrutiny in an adjudicative forum. (See also Standard 7.01, Professionalism, under Forensic Activities.)

1.24 Records and Data

Psychologists create, maintain, disseminate, store, retain, and dispose of records and data relating to their research, practice, and other work in accordance with law and in a manner that permits compliance with the requirements of this Ethics Code. (See also Standard 5.04, Maintenance of Records.)

1.25 Fees and Financial Arrangements

(a) As early as is feasible in a professional or scientific relationship, the psychologist and the patient, client, or other appropriate recipient of psychological services reach an agreement specifying the compensation and the billing arrangements.

(b) Psychologists do not exploit recipients of services or payors with respect to fees.

(c) Psychologists' fee practices are consistent with law.

(d) Psychologists do not misrepresent their fees.

(e) If limitations to services can be anticipated because of limitations in financing, this is discussed with the patient, client, or other appropriate recipient of services as early as is feasible. (See also Standard 4.08, Interruption of Services.)

(f) If the patient, client, or other recipient of services does not pay for services as agreed, and if the psychologist wishes to use collection agencies or legal measures to collect the fees, the psychologist first informs the person that such measures will be taken and provides that person an opportunity to make prompt payment. (See also Standard 5.11, Withholding Records for Nonpayment.)

1.26 Accuracy in Reports to Payors and Funding Sources

In their reports to payors for services or sources of research funding, psychologists accurately state the nature of the research or service provided, the fees or charges, and where applicable, the identity of the provider, the findings, and the diagnosis. (See also Standard 5.05, Disclosures.)

1.27 Referrals and Fees

When a psychologist pays, receives payment from, or divides fees with another professional other than in an employer–employee relationship, the payment to each is based on the services (clinical, consultative, administrative, or other) provided and is not based on the referral itself.

2. Evaluation, Assessment, or Intervention

2.01 Evaluation, Diagnosis, and Interventions in Professional Context

(a) Psychologists perform evaluations, diagnosis services, or interventions only within the context of a defined professional relationship. (See also Standard 1.03, Professional and Scientific Relationship.)

(b) Psychologists' assessments, recommendations, reports, and psychological diagnostic or evaluative statements are based on information and techniques (including personal interviews of the individual when appropriate) sufficient to provide appropriate substantiation for their findings. (See also Standard 7.02, Forensic Assessments.)

2.02 Competence and Appropriate Use of Assessments and Interventions

(a) Psychologists who develop, administer, score, interpret, or use psychological assessment techniques, interviews, tests, or instruments do so in a manner and for purposes that are appropriate in light of the research on or evidence of the usefulness and proper application of the techniques.

(b) Psychologists refrain from misuse of assessment techniques, interventions, results, and interpretations and take reasonable steps to prevent others from misusing the information these techniques provide. This includes refraining from releasing raw test results or raw data to persons, other than to patients or clients as appropriate, who are not qualified to use such information. (See also Standards 1.02, Relationship of Ethics and Law, and 1.04, Boundaries of Competence.)

2.03 Test Construction

Psychologists who develop and conduct research with tests and other assessment techniques use specific procedures and current professional knowledge for test design, standardization, validation, reduction or elimination of bias, and recommendations for use.

2.04 Use of Assessment in General and With Special Populations

(a) Psychologists who perform interventions or administer, score, interpret, or use assessment techniques are familiar with the reliability, validation, and related standardization or outcome studies of, and proper applications and uses of, the techniques they use.

(b) Psychologists recognize limits to the certainty with which diagnoses, judgments, or predictions can be made about individuals.

(c) Psychologists attempt to identify situations in which particular interventions or assessment techniques or norms may not be applicable or may require adjustment in administration or interpretation because of factors such as individuals' gender, age, race, ethnicity, national origin, religion, sexual orientation, disability, language, or socioeconomic status.

2.05 Interpreting Assessment Results

When interpreting assessment results, including automated interpretations, psychologists take into account the various test factors and characteristics of the person being assessed that might affect psychologists' judgments or reduce the accuracy of their interpretations. They indicate any significant reservations they have about the accuracy or limitations of their interpretations.

2.06 Unqualified Persons

Psychologists do not promote the use of psychological assessment techniques by unqualified persons. (See also Standard 1.22, Delegation to and Supervision of Subordinates.)

2.07 Obsolete Tests and Outdated Test Results

(a) Psychologists do not base their assessment or intervention decisions or recommendations on data or test results that are outdated for the current purpose.

(b) Similarly, psychologists do not base such decisions or recommendations on tests and measures that are obsolete and not useful for the current purpose.

2.08 Test Scoring and Interpretation Services

(a) Psychologists who offer assessment or scoring procedures to other professionals accurately describe the purpose, norms, validity, reliability, and applications of the procedures and any special qualifications applicable to their use.

(b) Psychologists select scoring and interpretation services (including automated services) on the basis of evidence of the validity of the program and procedures as well as on other appropriate considerations.

(c) Psychologists retain appropriate responsibility for the appropriate application, interpretation, and use of assessment instruments, whether they score and interpret such tests themselves or use automated or other services.

2.09 Explaining Assessment Results

Unless the nature of the relationship is clearly explained to the person being assessed in advance and precludes provision of an explanation of results (such as in some organizational consulting, preemployment or security screenings, and forensic evaluations), psychologists ensure that an explanation of the results is provided using language that is reasonably understandable to the person assessed or to another legally authorized person on behalf of the client. Regardless of whether the scoring and interpretation are done by the psychologist, by assistants, or by automated or other outside services, psychologists take reasonable steps to ensure that appropriate explanations of results are given.

2.10 Maintaining Test Security

Psychologists make reasonable efforts to maintain the integrity and security of tests and other assessment techniques consistent with law, contractual obligations, and in a manner that permits compliance with the requirements of this Ethics Code. (See also Standard 1.02, Relationship of Ethics and Law.)

3. Advertising and Other Public Statements

3.01 Definition of Public Statements

Psychologists comply with this Ethics Code in public statements relating to their professional services, products, or publications or to the field of psychology. Public statements include but are not limited to paid or unpaid advertising, brochures, printed matter, directory listings, personal resumes or curricula vitae, interviews or comments for use in media, statements in legal proceedings, lectures and public oral presentations, and published materials.

3.02 Statements by Others

(a) Psychologists who engage others to create or place public statements that promote their professional practice, products, or activities retain professional responsibility for such statements.

(b) In addition, psychologists make reasonable efforts to prevent others whom they do not control (such as employers, publishers, sponsors, organizational clients, and representatives of the print or broadcast media) from making deceptive statements concerning psychologists' practice or professional or scientific activities.

(c) If psychologists learn of deceptive statements about their work made by others, psychologists make reasonable efforts to correct such statements.

(d) Psychologists do not compensate employees of press, radio, television, or other communication media in return for publicity in a news item.

(e) A paid advertisement relating to the psychologist's activities must be identified as such, unless it is already apparent from the context.

3.03 Avoidance of False or Deceptive Statements

(a) Psychologists do not make public statements that are false, deceptive, misleading, or fraudulent, either because of what they state, convey, or suggest or because of what they omit, concerning their research, practice, or other work activities or those of persons or organizations with which they are affiliated. As examples (and not in limitation) of this standard, psychologists do not make false or deceptive statements concerning (1) their training, experience, or competence; (2) their academic degrees; (3) their credentials; (4) their institutional or association affiliations; (5) their services; (6) the scientific or clinical basis for, or results or degree of success of, their services; (7) their fees; or (8) their publications or research findings. (See also Standards 6.15, Deception in Research, and 6.18, Providing Participants With Information About the Study.)

(b) Psychologists claim as credentials for their psychological work, only degrees that (1) were earned from a regionally accredited educational institution or (2) were the basis for psychology licensure by the state in which they practice.

3.04 Media Presentations

When psychologists provide advice or comment by means of public lectures, demonstrations, radio or television programs, prerecorded tapes, printed articles, mailed material, or other media, they take reasonable precautions to ensure that (1) the statements are based on appropriate psychological literature and practice, (2) the statements are otherwise consistent with this Ethics Code, and (3) the recipients of the information are not encouraged to infer that a relationship has been established with them personally.

3.05 Testimonials

Psychologists do not solicit testimonials from current psychotherapy clients or patients or other persons who because of their particular circumstances are vulnerable to undue influence.

3.06 In-Person Solicitation

Psychologists do not engage, directly or through agents, in uninvited in-person solicitation of business from actual or potential psychotherapy patients or clients or other persons who because of their particular circumstances are vulnerable to undue influence. However, this does not preclude attempting to implement appropriate collateral contacts with significant others for the purpose of benefiting an already engaged therapy patient.

4. Therapy

4.01 Structuring the Relationship

(a) Psychologists discuss with clients or patients as early as is feasible in the therapeutic relationship appropriate issues, such as the nature and anticipated course of therapy, fees, and confidentiality. (See also Standards 1.25, Fees and Financial Arrangements, and 5.01, Discussing the Limits of Confidentiality.)

(b) When the psychologist's work with clients or patients will be supervised, the above discussion includes that fact, and the name of the supervisor, when the supervisor has legal responsibility for the case.

(c) When the therapist is a student intern, the client or patient is informed of that fact.

(d) Psychologists make reasonable efforts to answer patients' questions and to avoid apparent misunderstandings about therapy. Whenever possible, psychologists provide oral and/or written information, using language that is reasonably understandable to the patient or client.

4.02 Informed Consent to Therapy

(a) Psychologists obtain appropriate informed consent to therapy or related procedures, using language that is reasonably understandable to participants. The content of informed consent will vary depending on many circumstances; however, informed consent generally implies that the person (1) has the capacity to consent, (2) has been informed of significant information concerning the procedure, (3) has freely and without undue influence expressed consent, and (4) consent has been appropriately documented.

(b) When persons are legally incapable of giving informed consent, psychologists obtain informed permission from a legally authorized person, if such substitute consent is permitted by law.

(c) In addition, psychologists (1) inform those persons who are legally incapable of giving informed consent about the proposed interventions in a manner commensurate with the persons' psychological capacities, (2) seek their assent to those interventions, and (3) consider such persons' preferences and best interests.

4.03 Couple and Family Relationships

(a) When a psychologist agrees to provide services to several persons who have a relationship (such as husband and wife or parents and children), the psychologist attempts to clarify at the outset (1) which of the individuals are patients or clients and (2) the relationship the psychologist will have with each person. This clarification includes the role of the psychologist and the probable uses of the services provided or the information obtained. (See also Standard 5.01, Discussing the Limits of Confidentiality.)

(b) As soon as it becomes apparent that the psychologist may be called on to perform potentially conflicting roles (such as marital counselor to husband and wife, and then witness for one party in a divorce proceeding), the psychologist attempts to clarify and adjust, or withdraw from, roles appropriately. (See also Standard 7.03, Clarification of Role, under Forensic Activities.)

4.04 Providing Mental Health Services to Those Served by Others

In deciding whether to offer or provide services to those already receiving mental health services elsewhere, psychologists carefully consider the treatment issues and the potential patient's or client's welfare. The psychologist discusses these issues with the patient or client, or another legally authorized person on behalf of the client, in order to minimize the risk of confusion and conflict, consults with the other service providers when appropriate, and proceeds with caution and sensitivity to the therapeutic issues.

4.05 Sexual Intimacies With Current Patients or Clients

Psychologists do not engage in sexual intimacies with current patients or clients.

4.06 Therapy With Former Sexual Partners

Psychologists do not accept as therapy patients or clients persons with whom they have engaged in sexual intimacies.

4.07 Sexual Intimacies With Former Therapy Patients

(a) Psychologists do not engage in sexual intimacies with a former therapy patient or client for at least two years after cessation or termination of professional services.

(b) Because sexual intimacies with a former therapy patient or client are so frequently harmful to the patient or client, and because such intimacies undermine public confidence in the psychology profession and thereby deter the public's use of needed services, psychologists do not engage in sexual intimacies with former therapy patients and clients even after a two-year interval except in the most unusual circumstances. The psychologist who engages in such activity after the two years following cessation or termination of treatment bears the burden of demonstrating that there has been no exploitation, in light of all relevant factors, including (1) the amount of time that has passed since therapy terminated, (2) the nature and duration of the therapy, (3) the circumstances of termination, (4) the patient's or client's personal history, (5) the patient's or client's current mental status, (6) the likelihood of adverse impact on the patient or client and others, and (7) any statements or actions made by the therapist during the course of therapy suggesting or inviting the possibility of a posttermination sexual or romantic relationship with the patient or client. (See also Standard 1.17, Multiple Relationships.)

4.08 Interruption of Services

(a) Psychologists make reasonable efforts to plan for facilitating care in the event that psychological services are interrupted by factors such as the psychologist's illness, death, unavailability, or relocation or by the client's relocation or financial limitations. (See also Standard 5.09, Preserving Records and Data.)

(b) When entering into employment or contractual relationships, psychologists provide for orderly and appropriate resolution of responsibility for patient or client care in the event that the employment or contractual relationship ends, with paramount consideration given to the welfare of the patient or client.

4.09 Terminating the Professional Relationship

(a) Psychologists do not abandon patients or clients. (See also Standard 1.25e, under Fees and Financial Arrangements.)

(b) Psychologists terminate a professional relationship when it becomes reasonably clear that the patient or client no longer needs the service, is not benefiting, or is being harmed by continued service.

(c) Prior to termination for whatever reason, except where precluded by the patient's or client's conduct, the psychologist discusses the patient's or client's views and needs, provides appropriate pretermination counseling, suggests alternative service providers as appropriate, and takes other reasonable steps to facilitate transfer of responsibility to another provider if the patient or client needs one immediately.

5. *Privacy and Confidentiality*

These Standards are potentially applicable to the professional and scientific activities of all psychologists.

5.01 *Discussing the Limits of Confidentiality*

(a) Psychologists discuss with persons and organizations with whom they establish a scientific, or professional relationship (including, to the extent feasible, minors and their legal representatives) (1) the relevant limitations on confidentiality, including limitations where applicable in group, marital, and family therapy or in organizational consulting, and (2) the foreseeable uses of the information generated through their services.

(b) Unless it is not feasible or is contraindicated, the discussion of confidentiality occurs at the outset of the relationship and thereafter as new circumstances may warrant.

(c) Permission for electronic recording of interviews is secured from clients and patients.

5.02 *Maintaining Confidentiality*

Psychologists have a primary obligation and take reasonable precautions to respect the confidentiality rights of those with whom they work or consult, recognizing that confidentiality may be established by law, institutional rules, or professional or scientific relationships. (See also Standard 6.26, Professional Reviewers.)

5.03 *Minimizing Intrusions on Privacy*

(a) In order to minimize intrusions on privacy, psychologists include in written and oral reports, consultations, and the like, only information germane to the purpose for which the communication is made.

(b) Psychologists discuss confidential information obtained in clinical or consulting relationships, or evaluative data concerning patients, individual or organizational clients, students, research participants, supervisees, and employees, only for appropriate scientific or professional purposes and only with persons clearly concerned with such matters.

5.04 Maintenance of Records

Psychologists maintain appropriate confidentiality in creating, storing, accessing, transferring, and disposing of records under their control, whether these are written, automated, or in any other medium. Psychologists maintain and dispose of records in accordance with law and in a manner that permits compliance with the requirements of this Ethics Code.

5.05 Disclosures

(a) Psychologists disclose confidential information without the consent of the individual only as mandated by law, or where permitted by law for a valid purpose, such as (1) to provide needed professional services to the patient or the individual or organizational client, (2) to obtain appropriate professional consultations, (3) to protect the patient or client or others from harm, or (4) to obtain payment for services, in which instance disclosure is limited to the minimum that is necessary to achieve the purpose.

(b) Psychologists also may disclose confidential information with the appropriate consent of the patient or the individual or organizational client (or of another legally authorized person on behalf of the patient or client), unless prohibited by law.

5.06 Consultations

When consulting with colleagues, (1) psychologists do not share confidential information that reasonably could lead to the identification of a patient, client, research participant, or other person or organization with whom they have a confidential relationship unless they have obtained the prior consent of the person or organization or the disclosure cannot be avoided, and (2) they share information only to the extent necessary to achieve the purposes of the consultation. (See also Standard 5.02, Maintaining Confidentiality.)

5.07 Confidential Information in Databases

(a) If confidential information concerning recipients of psychological services is to be entered into databases or systems of records available to persons whose access has not been consented to by the recipient, then psychologists use coding or other techniques to avoid the inclusion of personal identifiers.

(b) If a research protocol approved by an institutional review board or similar body requires the inclusion of personal identifiers, such identifiers are deleted before the information is made accessible to persons other than those of whom the subject was advised.

(c) If such deletion is not feasible, then before psychologists transfer such data to others or review such data collected by others, they take reasonable steps to determine that appropriate consent of personally identifiable individuals has been obtained.

5.08 Use of Confidential Information for Didactic or Other Purposes

(a) Psychologists do not disclose in their writings, lectures, or other public media, confidential, personally identifiable information concerning their patients, individual or organizational clients, students, research participants, or other recipients of their services that they obtained during the course of their work, unless the person or organization has consented in writing or unless there is other ethical or legal authorization for doing so.

(b) Ordinarily, in such scientific and professional presentations, psychologists disguise confidential information concerning such persons or organizations so that they are not individually identifiable to others and so that discussions do not cause harm to subjects who might identify themselves.

5.09 Preserving Records and Data

A psychologist makes plans in advance so that confidentiality of records and data is protected in the event of the psychologist's death, incapacity, or withdrawal from the position or practice.

5.10 Ownership of Records and Data

Recognizing that ownership of records and data is governed by legal principles, psychologists take reasonable and lawful steps so that records and data remain available to the extent needed to serve the best interests of patients, individual or organizational clients, research participants, or appropriate others.

5.11 Withholding Records for Nonpayment

Psychologists may not withhold records under their control that are requested and imminently needed for a patient's or client's treatment solely because payment has not been received, except as otherwise provided by law.

6. *Teaching, Training Supervision, Research, and Publishing*

6.01 *Design of Education and Training Programs*

Psychologists who are responsible for education and training programs seek to ensure that the programs are competently designed, provide the proper experiences, and meet the requirements for licensure, certification, or other goals for which claims are made by the program.

6.02 *Descriptions of Education and Training Programs*

(a) Psychologists responsible for education and training programs seek to ensure that there is a current and accurate description of the program content, training goals and objectives, and requirements that must be met for satisfactory completion of the program. This information must be made readily available to all interested parties.

(b) Psychologists seek to ensure that statements concerning their course outlines are accurate and not misleading, particularly regarding the subject matter to be covered, bases for evaluating progress, and the nature of course experiences. (See also Standard 3.03, Avoidance of False or Deceptive Statements.)

(c) To the degree to which they exercise control, psychologists responsible for announcements, catalogs, brochures, or advertisements describing workshops, seminars, or other non-degree-granting educational programs ensure that they accurately describe the audience for which the program is intended, the educational objectives, the presenters, and the fees involved.

6.03 *Accuracy and Objectivity in Teaching*

(a) When engaged in teaching or training, psychologists present psychological information accurately and with a reasonable degree of objectivity.

(b) When engaged in teaching or training, psychologists recognize the power they hold over students or supervisees and therefore make reasonable efforts to avoid engaging in conduct that is personally demeaning to students or supervisees. (See also Standards 1.09, Respecting Others, and 1.12, Other Harassment.)

6.04 *Limitation on Teaching*

Psychologists do not teach the use of techniques or procedures that require specialized training, licensure, or expertise, including but not limited to hypnosis, biofeedback, and projective techniques, to individuals who lack the prerequisite training, legal scope of practice, or expertise.

6.05 Assessing Student and Supervisee Performance

(a) In academic and supervisory relationships, psychologists establish an appropriate process for providing feedback to students and supervisees.

(b) Psychologists evaluate students and supervisees on the basis of their actual performance on relevant and established program requirements.

6.06 Planning Research

(a) Psychologists design, conduct, and report research in accordance with recognized standards of scientific competence and ethical research.

(b) Psychologists plan their research so as to minimize the possibility that results will be misleading.

(c) In planning research, psychologists consider its ethical acceptability under the Ethics Code. If an ethical issue is unclear, psychologists seek to resolve the issue through consultation with institutional review boards, animal care and use committees, peer consultations, or other proper mechanisms.

(d) Psychologists take responsible steps to implement appropriate protections for the rights and welfare of human participants, other persons affected by the research, and the welfare of animal subjects.

6.07 Responsibility

(a) Psychologists conduct research competently and with due concern for the dignity and welfare of the participants.

(b) Psychologists are responsible for the ethical conduct of research conducted by them or by others under their supervision or control.

(c) Researchers and assistants are permitted to perform only those tasks for which they are appropriately trained and prepared.

(d) As part of the process of development and implementation of research projects, psychologists consult those with expertise concerning any special population under investigation or most likely to be affected.

6.08 Compliance With Law and Standards

Psychologists plan and conduct research in a manner consistent with federal and state law and regulations, as well as professional standards governing the conduct of research, and particularly those standards governing research with human participants and animal subjects.

6.09 Institutional Approval

Psychologists obtain from host institutions or organizations appropriate approval prior to conducting research, and they provide accurate information about their research proposals. They conduct the research in accordance with the approved research protocol.

6.10 Research Responsibilities

Prior to conducting research (except research involving only anonymous surveys, naturalistic observations, or similar research), psychologists enter into an agreement with participants that clarifies the nature of the research and the responsibilities of each party.

6.11 Informed Consent to Research

(a) Psychologists use language that is reasonably understandable to research participants in obtaining their appropriate informed consent (except as provided in Standard 6.12, Dispensing With Informed Consent). Such informed consent is appropriately documented.

(b) Using language that is reasonably understandable to participants, psychologists inform participants of the nature of the research; they inform participants that they are free to participate or to decline to participate or to withdraw from the research; they explain the foreseeable consequences of declining or withdrawing; they inform participants of significant factors that may be expected to influence their willingness to participate (such as risks, discomfort, adverse effects, or limitations on confidentiality, except as provided in Standard 6.15, Deception in Research); and they explain other aspects about which the prospective participants inquire.

(c) When psychologists conduct research with individuals such as students or subordinates, psychologists take special care to protect the prospective participants from adverse consequences of declining or withdrawing from participation.

(d) When research participation is a course requirement or opportunity for extra credit, the prospective participant is given the choice of equitable alternative activities.

(e) For persons who are legally incapable of giving informed consent, psychologists nevertheless (1) provide an appropriate explanation, (2) obtain the participant's assent, and (3) obtain appropriate permission from a legally authorized person, if such substitute consent is permitted by law.

6.12 Dispensing With Informed Consent

Before determining that planned research (such as research involving only anonymous questionnaires, naturalistic observations, or certain kinds of archival research) does not require the informed consent of research participants, psychologists consider applicable regulations and institutional review board requirements, and they consult with colleagues as appropriate.

6.13 Informed Consent in Research Filming or Recording

Psychologists obtain informed consent from research participants prior to filming or recording them in any form, unless the research involves simply naturalistic observations in public places and it is not anticipated that the recording will be used in a manner that could cause personal identification or harm.

6.14 Offering Inducement for Research Participants

(a) In offering professional services as an inducement to obtain research participants, psychologists make clear the nature of the services, as well as the risks, obligations, and limitations. (See also Standard 1.18 Barter [With Patients or Clients].)

(b) Psychologists do not offer excessive or inappropriate financial or other inducements to obtain research participants, particularly when it might tend to coerce participation.

6.15 Deception in Research

(a) Psychologists do not conduct a study involving deception unless they have determined that the use of deceptive techniques is justified by the study's prospective scientific, educational, or applied value and that equally effective alternative procedures that do not use deception are not feasible.

(b) Psychologists never deceive research participants about significant aspects that would affect their willingness to participate, such as physical risks, discomfort, or unpleasant emotional experiences.

(c) Any other deception that is an integral feature of the design and conduct of an experiment must be explained to participants as early as is feasible, preferably at the conclusion of their participation, but no later than at the conclusion of the research. (See also Standard 6.18, Providing Participants With Information About the Study.)

6.16 Sharing and Utilizing Data

Psychologists inform research participants of their anticipated sharing or further use of personally identifiable research data and of the possibility of unanticipated future uses.

6.17 Minimizing Invasiveness

In conducting research, psychologists interfere with the participants or milieu from which data are collected only in a manner that is warranted by an appropriate research design and that is consistent with psychologists' roles as scientific investigators.

6.18 Providing Participants With Information About the Study

(a) Psychologists provide a prompt opportunity for participants to obtain appropriate information about the nature, results, and conclusions of the research, and psychologists attempt to correct any misconceptions that participants may have.

(b) If scientific or humane values justify delaying or withholding this information, psychologists take reasonable measures to reduce the risk of harm.

6.19 Honoring Commitments

Psychologists take reasonable measures to honor all commitments they have made to research participants.

6.20 Care and Use of Animals in Research

(a) Psychologists who conduct research involving animals treat them humanely.

(b) Psychologists acquire, care for, use, and dispose of animals in compliance with current federal, state, and local laws and regulations, and with professional standards.

(c) Psychologists trained in research methods and experienced in the care of laboratory animals supervise all procedures involving animals and are responsible for ensuring appropriate consideration of their comfort, health, and humane treatment.

(d) Psychologists ensure that all individuals using animals under their supervision have received instruction in research methods and in the care, maintenance, and handling of the species being used, to the extent appropriate to their role.

(e) Responsibilities and activities of individuals assisting in a research project are consistent with their respective competencies.

(f) Psychologists make reasonable efforts to minimize the discomfort, infection, illness, and pain of animal subjects.

(g) A procedure subjecting animals to pain, stress, or privation is used only when an alternative procedure is unavailable and the goal is justified by its prospective scientific, educational, or applied value.

(h) Surgical procedures are performed under appropriate anesthesia; techniques to avoid infection and minimize pain are followed during and after surgery.

(i) When it is appropriate that the animal's life be terminated, it is done rapidly, with an effort to minimize pain, and in accordance with accepted procedures.

6.21 Reporting of Results

(a) Psychologists do not fabricate data or falsify results in their publications.

(b) If psychologists discover significant errors in their published data, they take reasonable steps to correct such errors in a correction, retraction, erratum, or other appropriate publication means.

6.22 Plagiarism

Psychologists do not present substantial portions or elements of another's work or data as their own, even if the other work or data source is cited occasionally.

6.23 Publication Credit

(a) Psychologists take responsibility and credit, including authorship credit, only for work they have actually performed or to which they have contributed.

(b) Principal authorship and other publication credits accurately reflect the relative scientific or professional contributions of the individuals involved, regardless of their relative status. Mere possession of an institutional position, such as Department Chair, does not justify authorship credit. Minor contributions to the research or to the writing for publications are appropriately acknowledged, such as in footnotes or in an introductory statement.

(c) A student is usually listed as principal author on any multiple-authored article that is substantially based on the student's dissertation or thesis.

6.24 Duplicate Publication of Data

Psychologists do not publish, as original data, data that have been previously published. This does not preclude republishing data when they are accompanied by proper acknowledgment.

6.25 Sharing Data

After research results are published, psychologists do not withhold the data on which their conclusions are based from other competent professionals who seek to verify the substantive claims through reanalysis and who intend to use such data only for that purpose, provided that the confidentiality of the participants can be protected and unless legal rights concerning proprietary data preclude their release.

6.26 Professional Reviewers

Psychologists who review material submitted for publication, grant, or other research proposal review respect the confidentiality of and the proprietary rights in such information of those who submitted it.

7. *Forensic Activities*

7.01 *Professionalism*

Psychologists who perform forensic functions, such as assessments, interviews, consultations, reports, or expert testimony, must comply with all other provisions of this Ethics Code to the extent that they apply to such activities. In addition, psychologists base their forensic work on appropriate knowledge of and competence in the areas underlying such work, including specialized knowledge concerning special populations. (See also Standards 1.06, Basis for Scientific and Professional Judgments; 1.08, Human Differences; 1.15, Misuse of Psychologists' Influence; and 1.23, Documentation of Professional and Scientific Work.)

7.02 *Forensic Assessments*

(a) Psychologists' forensic assessments, recommendations, and reports are based on information and techniques (including personal interviews of the individual, when appropriate) sufficient to provide appropriate substantiation for their findings. (See also Standards 1.03, Professional and Scientific Relationship; 1.23, Documentation of Professional and Scientific Work; 2.01, Evaluation, Diagnosis, and Interventions in Professional Context; and 2.05, Interpreting Assessment Results.)

(b) Except as noted in (c), below, psychologists provide written or oral forensic reports or testimony of the psychological characteristics of an individual only after they have conducted an examination of the individual adequate to support their statements or conclusions.

(c) When, despite reasonable efforts, such an examination is not feasible, psychologists clarify the impact of their limited information on the reliability and validity of their reports and testimony, and they appropriately limit the nature and extent of their conclusions or recommendations.

7.03 *Clarification of Role*

In most circumstances, psychologists avoid performing multiple and potentially conflicting roles in forensic matters. When psychologists may be called on to serve in more than one role in a legal proceeding—for example, as consultant or expert for one party or for the court and as a fact witness—they clarify role expectations and the extent of confidentiality in advance to the extent feasible, and thereafter as changes occur, in order to avoid compromising their professional judgment and objectivity and in order to avoid misleading others regarding their role.

7.04 *Truthfulness and Candor*

(a) In forensic testimony and reports, psychologists testify truthfully, honestly, and candidly and, consistent with applicable legal procedures, describe fairly the bases for their testimony and conclusions.

(b) Whenever necessary to avoid misleading, psychologists acknowledge the limits of their data or conclusions.

7.05 *Prior Relationships*

A prior professional relationship with a party does not preclude psychologists from testifying as fact witnesses or from testifying to their services to the extent permitted by applicable law. Psychologists appropriately take into account ways in which the prior relationship might affect their professional objectivity or opinions and disclose the potential conflict to the relevant parties.

7.06 *Compliance With Law and Rules*

In performing forensic roles, psychologists are reasonably familiar with the rules governing their roles. Psychologists are aware of the occasionally competing demands placed upon them by these principles and the requirements of the court system, and attempt to resolve these conflicts by making known their commitment to this Ethics Code and taking steps to resolve the conflict in a responsible manner. (See also Standard 1.02, Relationship of Ethics and Law.)

8. *Resolving Ethical Issues*

8.01 *Familiarity With Ethics Code*

Psychologists have an obligation to be familiar with this Ethics Code, other applicable ethics codes, and their application to psychologists' work. Lack of awareness or misunderstanding of an ethical standard is not itself a defense to a charge of unethical conduct.

8.02 *Confronting Ethical Issues*

When a psychologist is uncertain whether a particular situation or course of action would violate this Ethics Code, the psychologist ordinarily consults with other psychologists knowledgeable about ethical issues, with state or national psychology ethics committees, or with other appropriate authorities in order to choose a proper response.

8.03 Conflicts Between Ethics and Organizational Demands

If the demands of an organization with which psychologists are affiliated conflict with this Ethics Code, psychologists clarify the nature of the
conflict, make known their commitment to the Ethics Code, and to the
extent feasible, seek to resolve the conflict in a way that permits the fullest
adherence to the Ethics Code.

8.04 Informal Resolution of Ethical Violations

When psychologists believe that there may have been an ethical violation by another psychologist, they attempt to resolve the issue by bringing it to the attention of that individual if an informal resolution appears
appropriate and the intervention does not violate any confidentiality rights
that may be involved.

8.05 Reporting Ethical Violations

If an apparent ethical violation is not appropriate for informal resolution under Standard 8.04 or is not resolved properly in that fashion,
psychologists take further action appropriate to the situation, unless such
action conflicts with confidentiality rights in ways that cannot be resolved.
Such action might include referral to state or national committees on professional ethics or to state licensing boards.

8.06 Cooperating With Ethics Committees

Psychologists cooperate in ethics investigations, proceedings, and resulting requirements of the APA or any affiliated state psychological association to which they belong. In doing so, they make reasonable efforts
to resolve any issues as to confidentiality. Failure to cooperate is itself an
ethics violation.

8.07 Improper Complaints

Psychologists do not file or encourage the filing of ethics complaints
that are frivolous and are intended to harm the respondent rather than
to protect the public.

Index

Index of APA Ethical
Standards Citations

About the Editor

Rodney L. Lowman, PhD, currently serves as President of The Development Laboratories, a career assessment and industrial consulting organization, and, at the time of publication, as Department Head and Professor in the Department of Psychology and Behavioral Sciences at Louisiana Tech University. He has held adjunct or consulting faculty appointments in the Department of Psychology at Rice University and the Divisions of Medical Psychology and Occupational Medicine at Duke University Medical Center, and he served on the faculties of the University of Michigan and the University of North Texas, among others. He is a Fellow of the American Psychological Association (APA).

Dr. Lowman has been a prolific contributor to the professional literature. The author of six books and monographs, he has to date produced more than 60 scholarly publications. His books include *Counseling and Psychotherapy of Work Dysfunctions* (1993); *The Clinical Practice of Career Assessment: Interests, Abilities, and Personality* (1991); and *Pre-Employment Screening for Psychopathology: A Guide to Professional Practice* (1989).

In addition to his professional writing, Dr. Lowman has been active in training others in his approaches to career assessment and counseling. He has trained a large number of psychologists and other professionals in his interest-ability-personality career assessment models. His books are widely used in graduate teaching programs and are included in the collections of university libraries throughout the world.

Dr. Lowman has served on the APA's Committee on Psychological Tests and Assessments, on its Ethics Committee, and as Chair of its Board of Professional Affairs. He is past president of the Society of Psychologists in Management. He serves on the editorial boards of several scholarly journals and as editor of *The Psychologist-Manager Journal*. He received his PhD in Psychology from Michigan State University, specializing in Industrial/Organizational and Clinical Psychology, and he completed his Clinical Psychology internship at the Texas Research Institute of Mental Sciences.